Market Trends

Historical Data

Nigel Aksel

Second Edition

Nigel Aksel
Market Trends: Currencies, Bitcoin, Commodities, and Indices

2nd Edition
All Rights Reserved
ISBN: 9781087485362

Table of Content

List of Figures 4

List of Tables 5

List of Appendixes 6

Dedication 7

Introduction 8

Why market trends are so important? 9

Structure of the Book 10

Understanding market trends 11

Market Rules 17

Market Thinking 22

Market Analysis 24

EUR/USD 26

GBP/USD 30

JPY/USD 33

XAU/USD 36

Crude Oil WTI Futures 39

BTC/USD 43

S&P500 47

FTSE100 50

Asset Portfolio 53

Final Outcome 55

Ask yourself 57

List of Web-sites 58

Conclusion 59

About author 60

Appendix 61

Notes and Memories 98

List of Figures

Figure 1 Sample Table of Exchange Rate.. 13

Figure 2 Open and Close Prices for EUR/USD (1975 - 2019) 26

Figure 3 Max and Min Rates for EUR/USD (1975 - 2018)... 27

Figure 4 Differences Between Max and Min Rates for EUR/USD (1975 - 2018)....................... 28

Figure 5 Open and Close Rates for GPB/USD (1971 - 2019)....................................... 30

Figure 6 Max and Min Rates for GBP/USD (1971 - 2018)... 31

Figure 7 Differences Between Max and Min Rates for GBP/USD (1971 - 2018)....................... 32

Figure 8 Open and Close Rates for USD/JPY (1971 - 2019)....................................... 33

Figure 9 Max and Min Rates for USD/JPY (1971 - 2018)... 34

Figure 10 Differences Between Max and Min Rates for USD/JPY (1971 - 2018)....................... 35

Figure 11 Open and Close Prices for XAU/USD (1971 - 2019) 36

Figure 12 Max and Min Prices for XAU/USD (1971 - 2018) 37

Figure 13 Differences Between Max and Min Prices for XAU/USD (1971 - 2018) 38

Figure 14 Open and Close Prices for Crude Oil WTI Futures (1984 - 2019)........................... 39

Figure 15 Max and Min Prices for Crude Oil WTI Futures (1984 - 2018).................................. 40

Figure 16 Differences Between Max and Min Prices for Crude Oil WTI Futures (1984 - 2018)
.... 41

Figure 17 Open and Close Rates for BTC/USD (2012 - 2019)... 43

Figure 18 Max and Min Rates for BTC/USD (2012 - 2018)... 44

Figure 19 Differences Between Max and Min Rates for BTC/USD (2012 - 2018) 45

Figure 20 Open and Close Indicators for S&P500 (1971 - 2019)... 47

Figure 21 Max and Min Indicators for S&P500 (1971 - 2018).. 48

Figure 22 Differences Between Max and Min Indicators for S&P500 (1971 - 2018) 49

Figure 23 Open and Close Indicators for FTSE100 (2002 - 2019)... 50

Figure 24 Max and Min Indicators for FTSE100 (2002 - 2018)... 51

Figure 25 Differences Between Max and Min Indicators for FTSE100 (2002 - 2018).............. 52

List of Tables

Table 1 Characteristics of Market Trends.. 11
Table 2 Sample Table of Exchange Rate 13
Table 3 Description of the Sample Currency Rate.. 14
Table 4 Sample factor analysis and predications for Price Trend of the Product...................... 14
Table 5 Characteristics of Thinking in Various Trends 23
Table 6 Characteristics of Market Analysis 24
Table 7 Final Outcomes... 55

List of Appendixes

Appendix 1 Historical Data for EUR/USD (1975 – 2019) 61
Appendix 2 Historical Data for GBP/USD (1971 – 2019) 62
Appendix 3 Historical Data for USD/JPY (1971 – 2019) 63
Appendix 4 Historical Data for XAU/USD (1971 – 2019) 64
Appendix 5 Historical Data for Crude Oil WTI Futures (M) CFD (1984 – 2019) 65
Appendix 6 Historical Data for BTC/USD (2012 – 2019) 66
Appendix 7 Historical Data for S&P500 (1971 - 2019) 67
Appendix 8 Historical Data FTSE100 (2002 - 2019) 68
Appendix 9 Historical Data for AUD/USD (1971 - 2019) 69
Appendix 10 Historical Data for USD/RUB (1994 - 2019) 70
Appendix 11 Historical Data for USD/CHF (1971 - 2019) 71
Appendix 12 Historical Data for USD/CAD (1982 - 2019) 72
Appendix 13 Historical Data for USD/KZT (1995 - 2019) 73
Appendix 14 Historical Chart: Silver Futures (CFD) (1974 - 2019) 74
Appendix 15 Historical Chart: Crude Oil WTI Futures vs. USD/KZT (CFD) (1995 - 2018) 75
Appendix 16 EUR/GBP historical dynamics 76
Appendix 17 Working Hours of Markets 77
Appendix 18 Exchange Names, Abbreviations, Time Zones and Working Hours 78
Appendix 19 Top 30 Cryptocurrencies 79
Appendix 20 Historical Stock Prices of Amazon.com 80
Appendix 21 Historical Stock Prices of Apple Inc. 81
Appendix 22 List of S&P500 companies (07/18/2019) 82
Appendix 23 List of FTSE100 companies (07/19/2019) 93
Appendix 24 Sector and Industry Analysis of the United States 96
Appendix 25 Stock Portfolio 97

Dedication

This is a handbook and it is for everyone, who is interested to learn about trends and various currencies, cryptos, commodities, and indices.

If you are not a professional, it does not matter. You can easily understand the material to expand your horizon about various markets and their trends.

The purpose of the book is about my practical and analytical materials, as well as my personal ideas about the markets and trends. And you can always write to me for clarification and further improvements in the book.

This book is also dedicated to my kids. I believe that they have to learn the market trends first before they start anything in their life. And the earlier they learn them, the faster they will succeed in the area of profession.

One good point, today many professions are disappearing because of technological advancements and many more new professions are created, which many people do not know about. For example, you cannot imagine a work today without an IT specialist or SMM manager.

So, I structured the book for any young fellow. With the only idea in mind to make this book easy to read and understand using charts.

Enjoy reading and using the book as a reference!

I would be very grateful for any comment or feedback about the book.

Best wishes,

Nigel Aksel

Introduction

The market is changing every day. And it is better to feel it and understand it deeply to make your decision about the future.

I first started to analyze the markets when I was a student, more than 20 years ago. It was after reading several classical books, including by Theodor Dreiser "Financier" and by Leslie Elson Waller - "Banker". Reading these books a long time ago, I could understand how markets can influence bankers, economies and the world. So after, it was very important for me to understand the market first as it was a foundation for all areas of the economy. My old classical books definitely helped me to form an understanding about markets and actually my interest in marketing as my first specialization I selected during my bachelor.

Later, I read about 20 books in marketing, stock markets, currencies, and cryptos. But they were more technical and functional. So, I wanted something that I could use as a handbook for reviewing markets every day. I tried to gather materials for my reference book while trading and analyzing markets for many years.

Finally, the idea came to write this book about market trends. I decided to include all my tables and ideas I learned during my research and analysis. Besides, I included all the information and data about the main assets and securities. Moreover, I decided to write down some market rules and situations that I found as an influential factor for understanding markets.

I hope the book will be helpful for all readers, no matter of professional background. Most importantly it should become the reference tool, that you can continuously review and I am sure it will provide you with many ideas to define your growth in the future.

Why market trends are so important?

We live today in the era of trends.

We choose brand products based on positive trends in sales. We invest based on analysis of trends. We renovate our cities to meet the requirements of new trends of eco, smart and green cities. And practically, all activities are based on trends.

In fact, many characteristics of the market trends are simple. So, many people think that market trends are easy and require no knowledge and reading. But it is not.

For example, let's take a case when an investor asks you to invest one million US dollars in profitable business. In addition, he tells you that your earnings will depend on the successfulness of your investment. And another term is to return 100% of the investment if you fail with the trend. In many cases, most of the people have difficulty to agree. They will be unconfident about future trends. Even though they know the situation in the market well.

So, why markets trends are so important?

First, it relates to your future. The more positive the trend in the economy, the better the job you can find with the highest salary. And it means that you can earn a lot and save more for your future.

Second, it relates to your happiness. The more accurately you define the trends and make the right decision, the happier you will be.

Third, trends can be long-term, short term and deepening on timeframes. For example, you can notice a very high move up of your stock in the five 5-minute charts, but in the 1-day chart – it will be a downward trend.

Forth, trends can tell you about opportunities. For example, if you notice that there is a positive trend for gold, you can buy it with the purpose to get your opportunity.

Fifth, trends can tell you about risks in the market. The earlier you can understand that the prices will go down in 3-4 months, the more you will be prepared to meet the challenging issues.

Sixth, trends of indices can tell you about the business climate in the country. You can use it as an opportunity or you can decide on your investments etc.

Finally, trends require different strategies when markets are descending or ascending. So, if you do not know how to work with trends, you will only buy to play on high price, for example. But if you know the trends well, you can play on buying and selling depending on the trend's direction.

The last point shows that trends require different areas of knowledge to win in the market. Trends are exceptionally important to understand what knowledge you have to receive, gather or use in your life to successfully move in the trend direction.

Structure of the Book

The first idea about this book is to show markets trends in the way that you will understand how to predict the trends and know some specific factors.

There are many assets and securities in the market. And many of them are reliable and with high growth potential. And at the same time, there are many of them, which are penny or fraudulent. The idea was to show the trends of the main assets, which highly influence present international and local markets.

I selected the following pairs and assets:

1) EUR/USD
2) GBP/USD
3) USD/JPY
4) XAU/USD
5) Crude Oil/USD
6) BTC/USD
7) S&P500
8) FTSE100
9) USD/AUD
10) USD/CAD
11) USD/RUB
12) USD/CHF
13) USD/KZT

Historical data for all these pairs and assets you can find in the appendix of the book.

I was asking myself how to structure the book that it will become a reference book for specialists, marketers or traders and those who are starting their professional journey.

On the internet, you can find information about open/close, high and low prices, and in other market coefficients. They are helpful to see the market fluctuations necessary to predict the next trends.

The final point was where to start and how to finish a book so that a reader will gradually form an understanding and motivation to use this book as a handbook.

Therefore, the structure of the book has the following special sections:

1) My understanding of market trends;
2) Market Rules;
3) Market Thinking;
4) Market Analysis;
5) Market Forecast;
6) Useful Links;
7) Questions to ask;
8) Appendix etc.

Let's start from understanding basic ideas and concepts about the market trends.

Understanding market trends

Markets are similar to oceans. It has its own storms and quite days, calm and deep waves, sharks and carps, which create various trends.

In Table 1 you can easily understand market trends from various angles.

Table 1 Characteristics of Market Trends

Characteristics	Market Trends
Period	Long-Term, Mid-Term, Short Term
Types	Currency, Cryptocurrency, Commodity, Stocks, Bonds, ETFs, Funds, Agricultural products, Technology, Indices, etc.
Participants	Buyers and Sellers, Authorities, Brokers, Investors, Regulators, Central Banks, Governments
Direction	Up, Down, Flat, Zig-zag or Oscillating
Players	Bear - Bulls
Influential Factors	-News -Analytical data -Expert view and reviews -Top Management Role -Innovative products, solutions -Speculation -Statistical data -Consumer Power (sales, orders, demand) -Sellers (purchase, supply and etc.) -Economic indicators (inflation, unemployment, FDI, export, number of rigs, etc.) -Social indicators (taxation, preferences, subsidies, quotas, education, workforce conditions and training) -Financial factors (income, saving, personal investment, loans, etc.) -Historical data
Infrastructure and Technology	Exchanges, Markets, Blockchain, Auctions
Risks	Change of trend direction, flat trend, speculative trend, etc.
Market Trend Equilibrium	Demand=Supply
Market Trend Up and Down	Demand>Supply, Demand<Supply
Market Trend Evaluation Methodologies	-Technical analysis (equations, mathematical, chart, models), -Japanese candlesticks, -Historical data analysis -Chart history analysis -Fundamental analysis (news, company history, and profile, indicators), -Mathematical modeling

From Table 1 we can see many characteristics of the market trends. They provide us with an understanding of the market trends and, at the same time, with available resources and tools.

For example, you can see in the last row of Table 1 - market trend evaluation methodologies. Many traders and analysts will easily understand most of them. For instance, technical analysis and Japanese candlesticks are for those who want to trade effectively on short and midterm orders. Fundamental analysis is for those who want to build policies or invest in long-term projects. Mathematical models are for those, who want to understand the relationships of many variables of the market, which influence the trends. The last is important for policymaking and regulations.

The special focus of this book is historical data and chart history analysis. They are the simplest methodologies and they do not require any technical or business skills to learn.

Historical data analysis is about analyzing, comparing and understanding the past data of any market (e.g. currency, stock, crypto) and finding your market trend.

Chart history analysis is basically drawing and analyzing the charts based on gathered and inputted historical data.

Historical data analysis requires analytical skills to find the past data and develop an excel sheet to enter them in the right format. You can find sample tables for various assets in the appendix section Appendix (1-15).

Chart history analysis requires to create your working figures with available excel tools. You do not need to be an expert to create a chart. All you have to understand that your data in the right order and are correct to draw a chart.

To illustrate, let's imagine a chart and its characteristics.

The horizontal line is an indicator of time. The vertical line is always an indicator of your variable, for example, the market rate for EUR/USD.

The point, where two lines cross is a point of coordinates. It is a point, where time starts. For example, if you want to see the data for the last 10 years from 2000 to 2010. The point of coordinates should start from the year 2000. And each segment of the horizontal line will add one year. For example, the beginning of the next section will be 2001. And so on.

For vertical line – a crossing point is a 0 EUR/USD rate and it moves with similar segments to above. For larger sum pair rates, for example, USD/KZT rate, in which 1 USD equals 380 – one segment can be 10 KZT. For the EUR/USD rate, one segment of the vertical line can be 0,05 or 0,1 EUR.

To visualize effectively, it is important to see 2 variables where horizontal line is always TIME, and the vertical line is currency rate sum, production output or saving amount in monetary or physical terms.

REMEMBER! Time is a main variable of the trend line or direction, which is horizontal line

In the table format, for example, in the sample table below it is difficult to see the trend.

Table 2 Sample Table of Exchange Rate

Year	2000	2001	2002	2003	2004	2004	2005	2006	2007
Rate of currency	60	40	50	80	70	65	85	120	150

But in Figure 1, you can see the same numbers. And here you can easily define the rate and the trend.

Figure 1 Sample Table of Exchange Rate

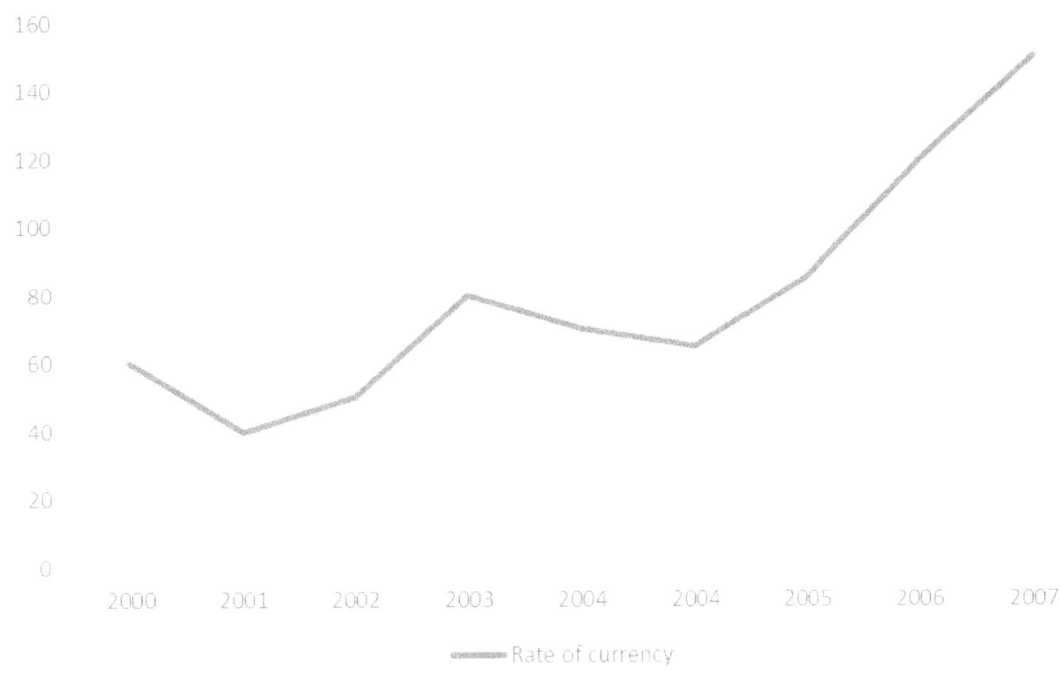

It is significant to understand that charts provide a better understanding of the trend. And the main aim is helping a reader to gather data in the proper way (Tables 1) and build the appropriate chart (Figure 1).

From Figure 1 we can see 2 descending and 2 ascending trends, and the general trend is ascending. We can also describe them in the table like in Table 3. But it takes additional lines.

Table 3 Description of the Sample Currency Rate

Year	2000	2001	2002	2003	2004	2004	2005	2006	2007
Rate of currency	60	40	50	80	70	65	85	120	150
Description of Trend in Section	Down	Up	Up	Up	Down	Up	Up	Up	Up
General Trend	Ascending								

So, most notably, it is better to understand how to read the tables and charts to define the trends. Generally, Figure 1 we saw above can be presented as a Table 2. In this, we can understand the data in the best way.

Another main point is to understand trends and predict the next trend. There are certain rules in technical analysis and standard forms of Japanese candlesticks that can give you a sign of predication. But they are not fixed rules and the final conditions depends on many other factors. To show the example, let's see Table 4.

Table 4 Sample factor analysis and predications for Price Trend of the Product

Price Trend of the Product	Factor analysis	Future price direction	Trend Prediction
Ascending	Demand is gradually increasing	Ascending further	Up
	Sales are gradually increasing	Ascending further	Up
	Company top management is changing	Descending possibility	Up
	Volumes are decreasing	Descending	Down
	Product complains	Descending possibility	Down
	Positive News about sales	Ascending possibility	Up
	Positive economic indicators	Ascending possibility	Down
Descending	News about a negative experience about the product	Descending further	Down
	The high rate of unemployment	Descending further	Up
	Shortages of delivery	Ascending possibility	Up
Flat	News about shortages of currency	Ascending possibility	Down
	Positive feedbacks on the media	Ascending possibility	Up

	The new finding of the harmful effects of the product	Descending	Down

In Table 4, we can see that there are many factors, which can influence the trend of the price for a certain product. No matter of the trend, we can see that future price's direction can sometimes do not match the trend predictions. There is no simple answer about the predications. It depends on many factors.

Neither technical analysis nor fundamental analysis can tell the exact direction of the trend.

First, many people base their judgments only on certain calculations. In many organizations, they simply add 10% growth for the next year, based on 10% growth in the last year. If the final growth will be 20% at the end of the coming year, they will never think that they could achieve 30-40% growth if they knew exactly what was the reason of the 10% growth last year. So, for effective prediction, it is important to gather and have data.

Second, many people base their predictions only on technical analysis. For example, a trader can base his predication on the model of the candles in the 1-day timeframe of analysis of the stocks. But on the weekly chart, the situation can be totally opposite. So, it is important to check the other factors, which is out of the timeframe fluctuations.

Third, many people base their forecast only on fundamental analysis. For example, a company can base its prediction on the analysis of the economic indicators of the country. But, in the fast-changing global environment, the actual product price of the company is based on the price changes of the foreign market's demand or its indicators or simply demand and supply.

Forth, predication is a proposed scenario. It is not the final case. No matter how we are good at analysis, predication is not exactly the fact. Usually, factual data is more or less than predicted.

The book helps you to understand an important lesson of the market trends by constant predictions based on your skills. The more you practice and learn the subject well, the more your predictions will be exact and true.

So, the final understanding is about how to predict closer to the possible scenario. In order to be good at prediction, it is important to do the following:

1) Learn the topic or asset well from different angles.
2) Understand the historical data.
3) Draw charts.
4) Compare with other indicators and prices.
5) Analyze the market data.
6) Analyze various scenarios and stakeholders.
7) Understand the market rules.

No matter of your skills, the most important is to understand the market rules. When you will understand how markets work - you understand how markets behave. You will easily find the best model to do a closer prediction.

Market Rules

It is well known that in any area, culture or specialization there are certain rules. If you do not follow rules, you can put yourself in a big danger or risk.

To illustrate, you have to keep your helmet in the construction site. And it rules for all. Or at the airport, you have to be two hours before the flight time, otherwise, you will be late to find your airline rack or your flight gate. And it also can take more time in the passport or customs control depending on the country of your flight. The same with the university, in order to get your diploma, you have to finish all your credit subjects and get your scores. This kind of rules is everywhere. And even at home or family, you have your own rules where to put your shoes, clothes or park your car, etc.

Rules keep people well-organized, on time, effective and successful. The stronger the rules, the more disciplined and purposeful a person.

For example, in the military or in sports, rules are very strict for your time schedule, nutrition, physical activities, and sleeping. And we can see that soldiers are more organized, disciplined and purposeful even though they did not receive enough of intellectual knowledge.

In the markets, there are rules that are compulsory and strict to follow in order to understand, grow and succeed. These rules are unique rules of the markets, like in many examples above. When you get an understanding of those rules, it will be much easier to see and define your trends.

In this book, I decided to share the rules from my own experiences. These rules keep me efficient in any market condition and trend. Let's check them out.

Rule 1: Market prices fluctuate based on demand and supply and its volumes.

For example, if demand is higher than supply, then the prices will go up.

If demand is decreasing than prices will drop low.

If supply is decreasing than prices will go up.

If demand is increasing then prices will increase.

If supply is increasing then prices will go down.

The equilibrium price is a point where supply equals demand.

Rule 2: Markets are open for buyers and sellers, to satisfy demand, but they are open also for an intermediary, for those who speculate or buy to resell them.

Markets are really for everyone. You can work there when you are comfortable, many markets are open almost 5 days a week. But with time zone, it is almost 6 days a week.

Cryptocurrency markets are open 24 hours and 7 days a week.

For many traders and people around the world various markets, especially with online trade tools, create many opportunities to work 24/7.

Rule 3: Markets require understanding, patience, and wisdom for investment.

For many people markets are also a place for investment. Today, many products do not need a physical purchase of the good or raw. For example, Crude Oil. You can invest by selling to earn on descending or buying to earn on ascending prices.

Rule 4: Markets require planning for actions.

Without understanding historical data and trends, any action can create a high risk for your trading, investment. If you buy for consumption by your business, you will be still at risk when you buy the commodity without planning.

Today, there are a lot of trading and investment platforms with virtual money. You can learn there, honing your skills in planning and working in the market.

For example, I use Investopedia.com. It has a very good simulator to test your planning and trading in the stock market.

Rule 5: Use technology for analysis and creating charts

Markets have a long history. Many people learned a big lesson and succeeded in the market and there are a lot of those who failed. Markets require constant analysis of data, prices, indices, volumes and etc. You have to use technology, which is available on every computer.

For example, Excel can become a useful tool. It is a standard tool and it allows you to analyze data and create charts.

Rule 6: Save money to enter the markets

For entering markets, you have to learn how to save money or resource. Otherwise, you can leverage your credit money in the trading and investment markets. But it will be too risky to trade and invest in mid-term and long-term trends.

With saved capital, you can buy or sell the stocks, indices, cryptos and still keep them in your account for future trends.

Rule 7: Collaborate with money experts and investors

Markets are like oceans, where you have both sharks and seals. Similarly, markets have peaks and bottoms, which are created by market volatility, speculation and many other events in various parts of the world.

It requires a lot of knowledge, which is not for remembering, but for articulating and thinking about relationships and their contradictory effects on your capital.

Collaborating with money experts and investors will help you to share unique experiences and learn something new about trends and situations that can be useful for investing or trading, and mainly avoid unexpected risks.

Rule 8: Learn and educate yourself about markets

Markets are very dynamic and it changes really quickly. You can have 100 reasons that the prices will go up, but it will actually go down, only because of one reason.

To understand the market, you have to learn all the time. You have to analyze prices, volumes, events, etc.

You can also learn technical skills.

There are a lot of books, which provide you with the best knowledge to understand the market and its trends.

Rule 9: Create a portfolio

Markets are volatile. If some positions go up, some positions go down. And vice versa.

To be on your safe side, when you are entering markets for investment or trading, you have to learn how to diversify your investment by creating a portfolio.

You can invest in stocks, cryptocurrencies, currencies, commodities and other assets at the same time.

Rule 10: Never do your decisions on emotions and unrealistic dreams

Markets are not the dream tool or place for regrets and offenses.

Markets are places for meeting buyers or sellers, and the main aim is to stay win-win in every deal.

Markets do not act to realize your unrealistic dreams to be rich in one day or help you to make you happy by buying something.

Remember always the rule No 1.

Rule 11: Develop a risk plan for the market

Markets are merciless. They move toward equilibrium when demand meets the supply. This is again the rule number one.

It means a market moves always to a point when both buyers and sellers are happy. Only at the point of the deal. Future time is a point for more happiness or sadness. And nobody knows how the trend can change.

Therefore, prepare your risk plan.

For example, for invested USD 100, you can be ready for the risk of USD20-30 maximum. For the case, if the market does not work for you, you close your order with your maximum risk amount. This is, however, when you trade with leverage.

Rule 12: Start your portfolio with assets you really understand

If you are not sure, do not start. Start better with assets you are familiar with from your past experience, education, analysis, or someone from your family members or friends are working in this business.

You have to ask some questions yourself such as: "Do I really know where I am investing?" or "Is it just because everyone is investing?". If you are not sure about the assets and their history, you are going to have a very serious headache. You will lose your money, time and nerves. So, never do it like that.

Rule 13: Control yourself and your emotions.

Even in the worse scenario, for example, when you lose all your money or capital in the market – control yourself and your emotions! Take it as a lesson. Understand what and where you did wrong.

Never give up. Stay focused on your main and long-term goals.

The most important asset is your brain. If you learn how to use it effectively, you will quickly recover from your loss.

Rule 14: Monitor your portfolio every day.

Check your portfolio, important news, and market information and make decisions appropriately.

You do not need to trade or invest or re-invest every day. You have to read the news, analyze historical data, check your portfolio and follow your prices, where they are heading.

Rule 15: Diversify your activities

Focus on your markets and follow the trends. But at the same time, do your lovely jobs as well.

You can find many jobs for your harmony, creativity, and income. It will take your attention from the market.

For example, you can open a restaurant, online magazine, or become a designer of various clothes or underwear. There are a lot of areas to approach your market, which will support you in your decisions.

Rule 16: Learn trends from different angles

Trends have many factors, which influence the directions positively or negatively to your budget.

Generally, trend factors can be classified as:

1) Strong
2) Medium
3) Weak

As an expert, you have to learn which factors are strong to influence the market trends. It will help you to monitor the factors and take adequate actions.

Rule 17: Adapt to market, never go against it.

If you see a disruptive change, try to adapt to the market. It means that some new technology or concept is on the horizon. It can be also a new regulation.

So, try to adapt to market changes. Never try to go against it. For example, if the prices are going down, never buy it without understanding.

Rule 18: Make your decision yourself.

There are a lot of statistics that almost 80-90% of the marketers are always losing their money or are at high risk.

Taking into account, please make your decision yourself based on your analyzed data.

It will save you from blaming or from emotions. You will take it as your experience, not anybody's else.

Rule 19: Start the analysis of historical data.

Always start the analysis from historical data. From past data, you will understand all about the trends and what the chances for your success in the market. You can also predict future trends with a better probability.

The purpose of this book is to show you more historical data.

Rule 20: Enter and exit markets in the right trends.

In the markets, up to 90% of the people lose because of fluctuations. So, understand this and increase your chances of winning the market.

You have to learn when to enter the market and when to exit.

Stay positive and follow the 20 rules constantly to achieve the goal!

These are my 20 rules for every day and they can help anyone to stay focused on market trends.

Rules can also strengthen your market thinking and help you to achieve new market goals.

Market Thinking

There are many countries where people have still old thinking. They believe that markets are running based on orders of the governor or the president. For example, in many countries, a majority part of companies is still state-owned. For example, Kazakhstan and any former soviet country are in this row, except Baltic countries.

On the other hand, in many parts of the world, countries take a development model and use it for many years until the state goes bankrupt or goes into recession. It influences the internal markets and economic conditions of the people.

In fact, many countries need market thinking. It is a very demanding topic as it means that people have to learn to live and win in the market trend.

Generally, the main principles of market thinking are:

1) Learn and win in any market trend;
2) Adapt to market conditions;
3) Change and develop to lead the markets;
4) Innovate to preserve in the market;
5) Accept losses as a lesson and to be a stronger marketer.

Market thinking is not only a process of understanding, analysis, and articulation of market concepts but also a strong attitude of focusing on long-term results and growth.

Kazakhstan has only 28 years of independence and it is too short time to form a new generation of people with market thinking. For example, the US has more than 300 years of experience in independence and forming market thinking.

This is one of the reasons that many reforms are short term and has so many problems in their realization at the present time.

Many experts say that there is no chance of developing without experience. However, this is not true. Humans have the best qualities so that they can learn from the experience of other people or countries.

To illustrate, any person can learn the language without being born in the native country. After learning, some international people can speak the language better than local people. That's the brain of people that control the development and thinking.

The same with market thinking. People and countries can learn the experience of countries by reading and learning the specific literature, statistics, and history, etc.

Definitely, there are some solutions that could help any country or person to accelerate the learning of new skills about how to expand market thinking in any environment. They are the following:

1) Learning a language of the most market developed economies;
2) Visiting a country as a tourist;
3) Comparative analysis of countries;

4) Critical thinking about present policies and drawbacks;
5) Exchange programs to expand knowledge about the country, people, etc.
6) Training programs to learn about market thinking of the leading country.
7) Participation in the conferences and forums;
8) Following market experts;
9) Reading books etc.

Analyzing various scenarios in the markets one can see that on different stages of the market trends, there are various behaviors. The behavior usually depends on thinking.

To illustrate, let us check the following Table 5.

Table 5 Characteristics of Thinking in Various Trends

	Uptrend	Highest Point	Down Trend	Lowest Point	Flat
Investor Thinking	Invest	Invest and Take profit when low	Invest and take profit at a lower point	Invest and take profit when high	Wait and analyze
Trader Thinking	Buy	Invest by selling, Take profit	Sell	Invest by buying, take profit	Analyze and Sell or Buy
Traditional Thinking	Invest by buying	Take profit	Wait	Wait	Wait
Market thinking	Earn on-trend, Adapt to trend	Take profit, prepare for a downtrend	Earn on-trend, adapt to the trend	Take profit, prepare for an uptrend	Screen and analyze, be ready for the trend

Market thinking people are close to investor and trader thinking people. Because they are the one who can use up and downtrends effectively by adapting and taking its advantages.

Traditional thinking people have their limitations. And from observation, many traditional thinking people are thinking and waiting for only upward trends. They simply do not know how to behave in the downward or flat trends.

There are many ways as mentioned to improve market thinking, but not everyone can become a trader or investor. At the same time, building the market thinking does not mean to learn how to invest or trade. For example, a biology teacher of the school should not worry about how to invest or trade. But, to be on the safe side, a biology teacher can develop a market thinking. It will help to adapt to various fluctuations in the economy, simply by saving and adapting to various conditions.

Adaption is an attitude and process and it is really important to be strong psychologically. It is important for anyone to learn how to live without panic in downtrends and recognize the market bottoms as a temporary period.

Therefore, it is important to analyze the markets constantly.

Market Analysis

From its definitions, market analysis is a process of evaluation of market conditions and trends.

Table 6 shows various types of market analysis with characteristics over purpose, development and interesting side.

Table 6 Characteristics of Market Analysis

	MARKET ANALYSIS		
	Purpose	**Development**	**Interested side**
Marketing Analysis	Define markets and customers	Company, Product, Customers, Partners, Stakeholders	Company
SWOT Analysis	Strategy building	Company, Product	Company
PEST Analysis	Strategy building	Company, Product	Company
Benchmarking	Study the best features of competitive companies or products	Company, Product	Company
Investment Feasibility Study	Study the possibility and profitability for the realization of the project	Project, Product, Investment	Investor
Technical Analysis	Predict market price and invest	Securities, Stocks, CFD, currencies, cryptocurrencies	Trader
Candlestick Analysis	Predict market price and invest	Securities, Stocks, CFD, currencies, cryptocurrencies	Trader
Competitor Analysis	Define and evaluate competitors	Company, Product	Company
Customer Analysis	Define customers and products	Customer, Product	Company
Fundamental Analysis	Evaluate markets	Investment, Industry, Economy	Company, Investor
Risk Analysis	Evaluate the risks of the company	The company, Investment, Project	Company, Investor
Target Market Analysis	Define and evaluate the target market	Product, Customer	Company

From the table, we can see that when we talk about market research, it is generally a broader topic. Depending on the type of market research, it differentiates based on the purpose, development and interesting side.

When we talk about any market, it is too general.

Therefore, it is better to start a market analysis from the following point:

1) Defining the target goal. For example, questions to ask can include: What am I going to do? Trade or invest? Develop a product or launch a project?

2) Defining the target market. For example, questions to ask are: Who are my customers? How can I learn about my customers? Where do they live? What do they drink?
3) Select the best methodology for market analysis from Table 6.
4) Use the internet to access quickly to databases.
5) Use online investment and trading platforms for analysis of markets.
6) Prepare the excel or online tables for data entry and constant analysis.
7) Create charts to visualize your data.
8) Analyze the reasons for changes, trends, ups, downs, reverse moves.
9) Mark them on your charts and add comments in the tables.
10) Check the latest news, events in the market.
11) Predict the market trend for the short, mid and long terms.
12) Check your data and predict.
13) Evaluate your market knowledge and predictions.
14) Use your market knowledge and thinking about investing and trading.

There are many types of markets indeed. And the book helps to show examples of analysis and how to make predictions with the main market information and charts in the coming sections.

EUR/USD

EUR/USD is the most traded currency in the world. The Forex nickname for the pair is Fiber. This pair represents the world's largest economies - the US and the EU. Even though the Euro appeared in the market in late 1998, the history of EUR/USD started in 1975 as a digital currency.

According to the Bank of International Settlements, the EUR/USD pair accounts for more than 23% of all transactions.

In Figure 2, you can see the historical graph of open and close rates for the EUR/USD pair.

Figure 2 Open and Close Prices for EUR/USD (1975 - 2019)

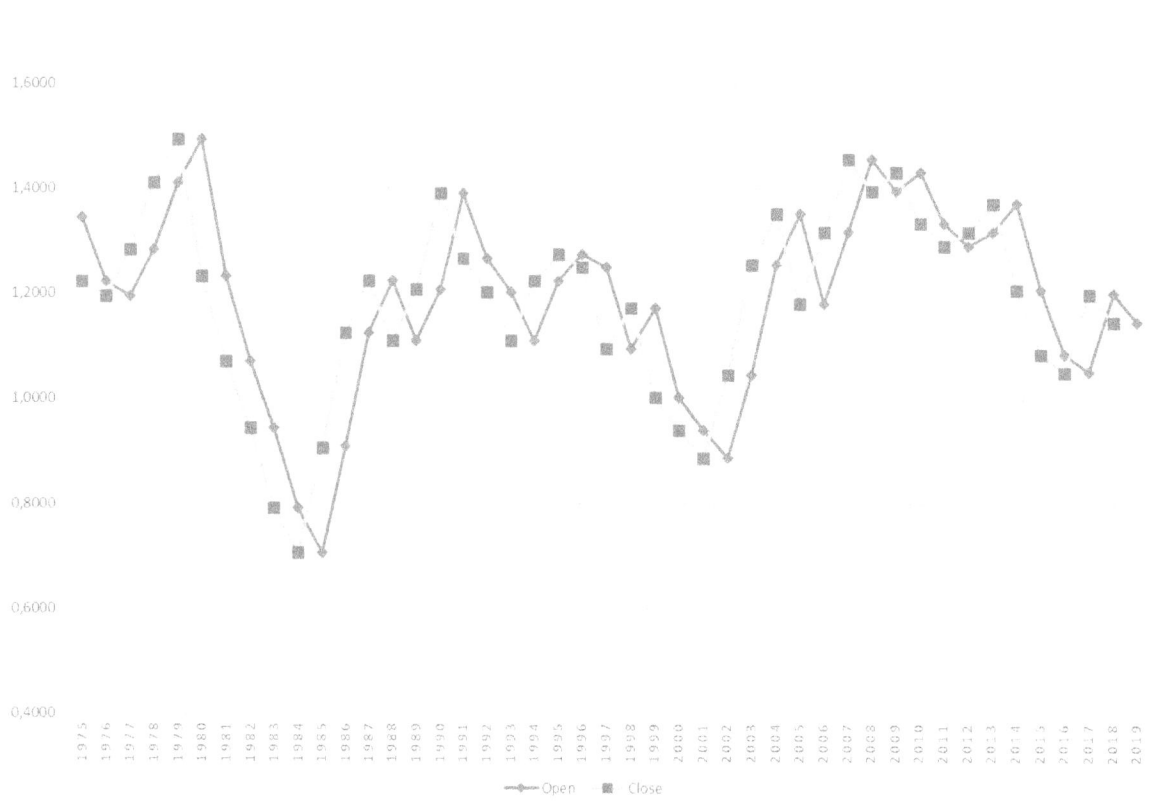

From Figure 2, we can see that EUR/USD pair fluctuates from its beginning period. And there were 3 peaks and 3 bottoms in the period from 1975 to 2019.

From the graph, we can see that the rates for pair are in the medium and is in the downturn trend.

However, in 2019 the US President pointed out several times that the US is going to devaluate the dollar to improve the competitiveness of the American products.

Taking into account, we can say that the pricing will be up to 1.4 from the year 2019 till 2022.

In addition, let's see the max and min price changes for the EUR/USD pair from the period 1975 to 2018 (in Figure 3).

Figure 3 Max and Min Rates for EUR/USD (1975 - 2018)

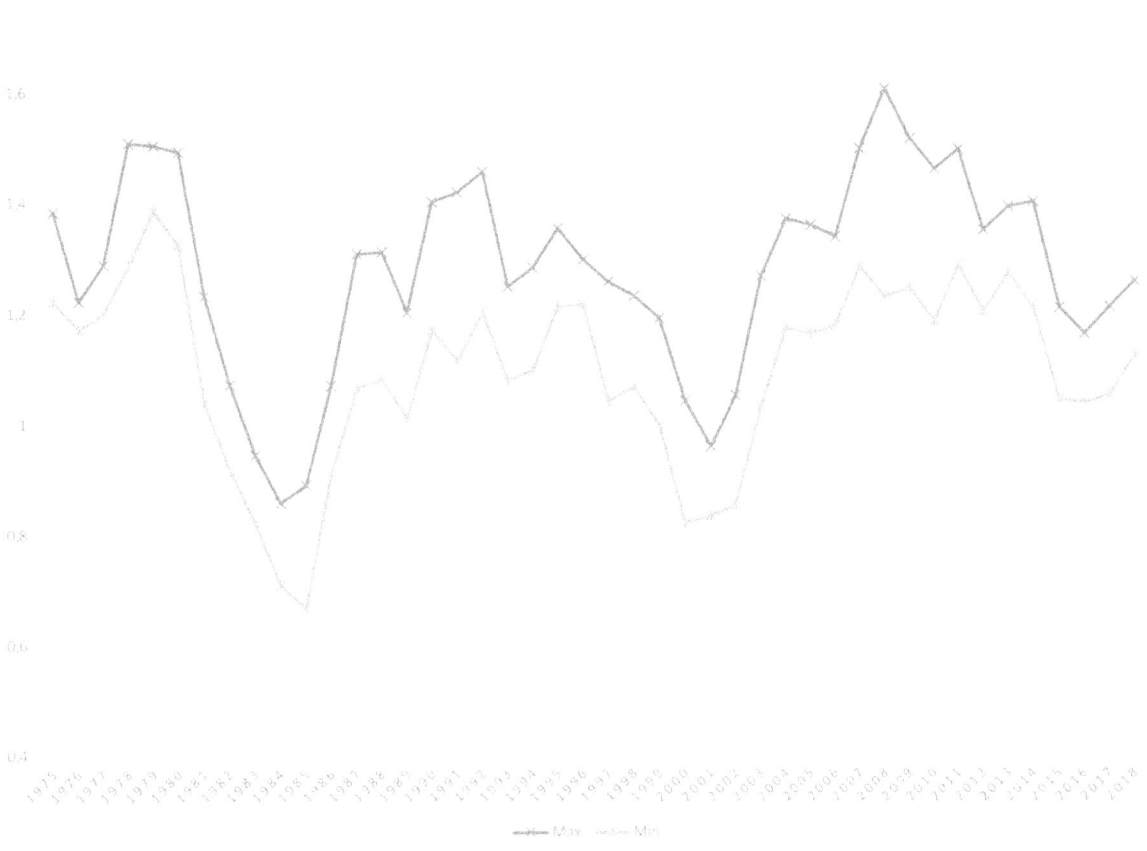

From Figure 3, we can see that the price trend goes up. The ascending trend can also be as a result of Donald Trump's trade policy to protect American businesses.

Another main point, from Figure 3, we can see 3 bottoms in the ascending trend. And we can see also that the downward trend is finished and formed in 2016-2017 the third bottom.

All these show that the trend of the EUR/USD for coming years will be ascending (if you connect 3 bottoms, you will see the upward trend). Generally, it means that USD will be weakening and the euro will be strengthening its value in the midterm period.

Now let's check what influences the EUR/USD rate. They are:

1) Supply and Demand for European Goods and Services. The more demand comes for EU good and services, the higher the demand for EUR. It will usually strengthen EUR;
2) Demand for EUR. Demand for EUR comes also from tourists. The more they visit EU, the higher the demand for EUR. That is also strengthening EUR;

3) Central Bank Monetary Policies. The Central Bank regulates the currency volume and its rate to make EU products and services more competitive. So, to meet the demand, it supplies an additional amount of EUR into account or provides loans to the countries to purchase EU goods and services;

4) Economic Indicators. There are many indicators, which influence the currency. For example, the unemployment level or export volume. If the economic conditions worsen in the EU, then it is a sign that there are not so many tourists are coming or many goods are exporting from the EU. And it weakens the EUR;

5) Political Decisions. Political decisions of one country can influence the currency in many ways. For example, EU Trade War with US or EU sanctions to Russia. These are the political steps that decrease the export of goods and services from the EU or limit tourists. As a result, all is going to weaken EUR.

Besides, in 2018, the World Bank reported that the GDP of the US is equal to 20,5 trillion US dollars and the GDP of the EU is around 18,7 trillion US dollars. And both countries' GDP is more than 45% of the global GDP.

This factor makes EUR/USD pair the most attractive, liquid and at the same time the most speculative currency in the world.

Figure 4 Differences Between Max and Min Rates for EUR/USD (1975 - 2018)

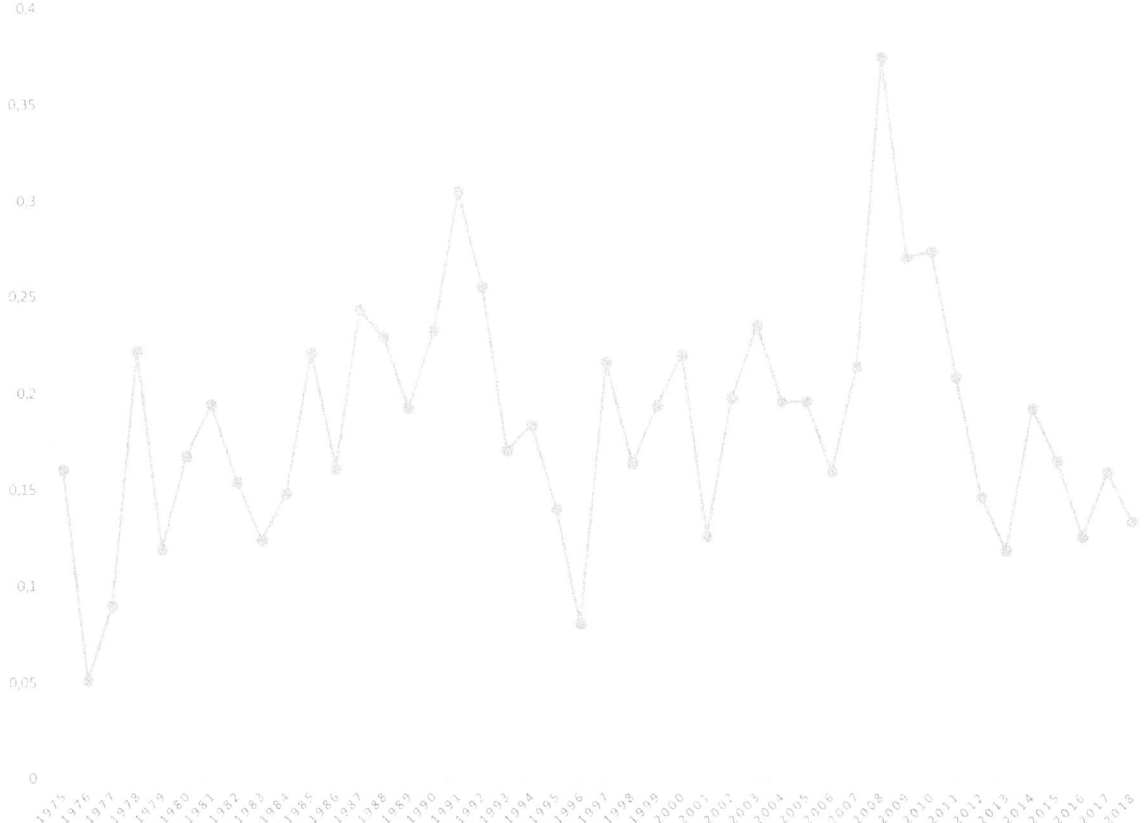

In Figure 4, we can see the fluctuation of the annual rate difference, which creates ample opportunities for currency traders, marketers and investors.

At the same time, Figure 4 shows the fading fluctuations of the downward trend. So, it can be a sign that the US dollar will be weakening in the coming years.

Generally, all three figures above show a starting ascending market trend.

What could it mean?

1) The USD will be weakening.
2) The EUR will be strengthening.
3) The competitiveness of the US market will be increasing.
4) European markets will have new challenges

There are many other factors, which can bring reverse effects. The main of them can be the following:

1) US-China Trade Wars, which will decrease the trade volume between two countries, but increase a trading volume in directions EU-US and EU-China.
2) US-Mexico Border Control, which will decrease the export of the American goods and services to Mexico.
3) Stagnation in Europe can cause lower imports from the US. The reasons for stagnation can come from sanctions to Russia and some other key trade partners.

At the same time, trade conflict cases with some countries such as China, Russia, Iran can boost the trade volumes of the US and EU with India, South-East Asia, Central Asian countries, Middle East, Africa, Latin America and etc.

Generally, the historical data can tell you a lot of other details.

For additional research of historical data for EUR/USD (1975-2019), you can check out the Appendix 1.

GBP/USD

The GBP/USD is the next well-known currency pair, which is one of the oldest. The Forex nickname for GBP is "Cable". But the British pound has many other names such as Pound Sterling, Sterling, Quid, and Nicker.

The popularity of the British Pound is in its old history and GB's role in the world financial trade.

We can see that the GBP/USD pair has a downward trend for more than 10 years (Figure 5). It means that the GBP was weakening.

Figure 5 Open and Close Rates for GPB/USD (1971 - 2019)

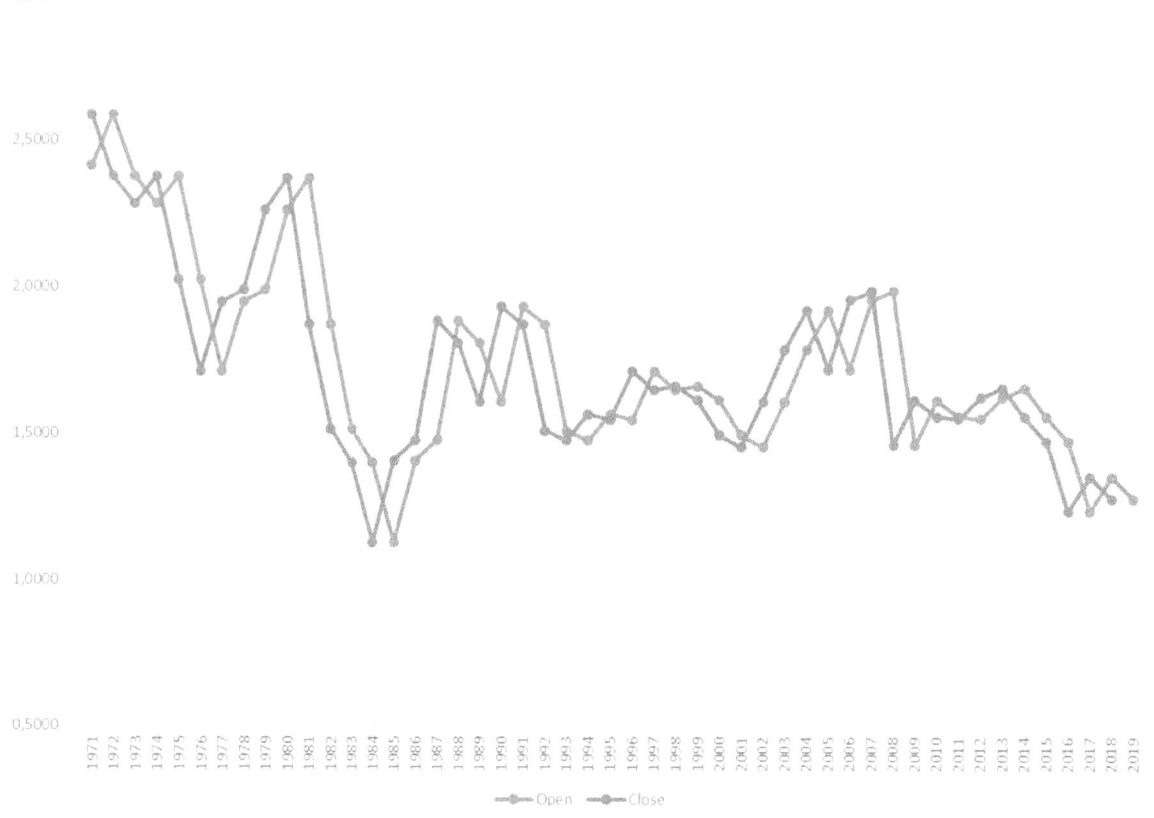

From Figure 5, we can notice that USD was strengthening.

However, if we check the EUR/GBP chart (Appendix 16), we can see that GBP was strengthening from 2016.

This shows that UK goods are more competitive in the US than in the EU area. The one reason, the UK has difficulty with trading and building relations with the EU zone. For example, events related to Brexit strongly influenced the UK currency.

One of the main reasons would be:

1) The US is more trading now with EU countries;

2) EU is the largest economy with more than 500 million citizens and is more attractive to American companies;
3) EU has open borders with the UK but there are different currencies;
4) EU has many countries, with low-level income and high level of migration.

And this is the main point why GBP/USD will further go down in the future. It will gradually be a descending trend.

Figure 6, shows max and min prices for GPB/USD. Despite the fact, that we can see an upward trend from 2017, we can also notice a bigger downward trend, which is started in 2007 and is still not finished.

Figure 6 Max and Min Rates for GBP/USD (1971 - 2018)

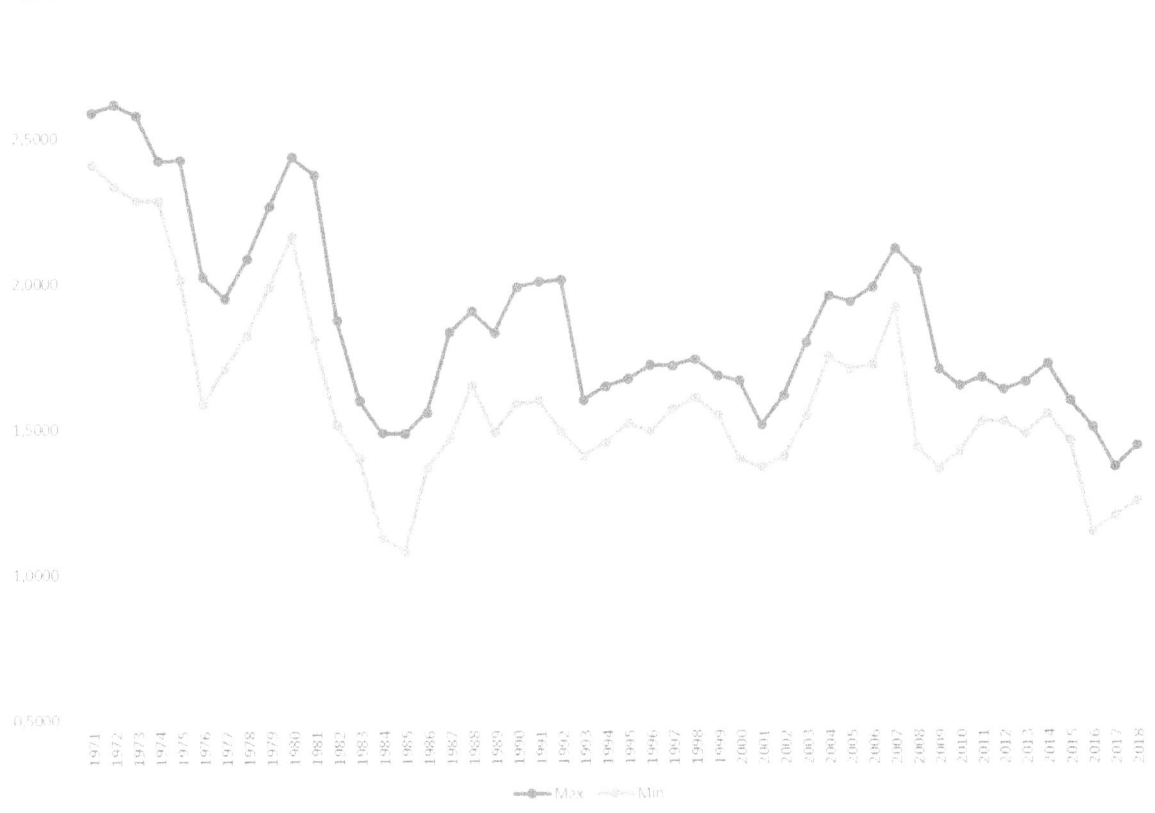

We can also notice this from Figure 7. Here, we can see the fading fluctuation of max and min prices. Here, the chart shows the descending trend of differences from 2009.

The main reasons for the downward trend of the pair are:

1) UK economy is only 13% of the US economy and 14% of the EU economy.
2) GBP increases its currency value by Brexit, but, at the same time, it becomes less competitive than the EU and the US.
3) Less competitiveness means a higher risk of stagnation.
4) Higher risk of stagnation can cause the devaluation of the GBP currency in the long-run.

What are the main directions that the UK can preserve its status as the global financial center?

1) UK can benefit from expansion in the EU zone. The volume of the trade can be 2-3 times higher than the volume of trade with the US.
2) The cryptocurrency market is booming. Many currencies are already becoming a firm investment solution. The UK can utilize this to lead the trend.

Figure 7 Differences Between Max and Min Rates for GBP/USD (1971 - 2018)

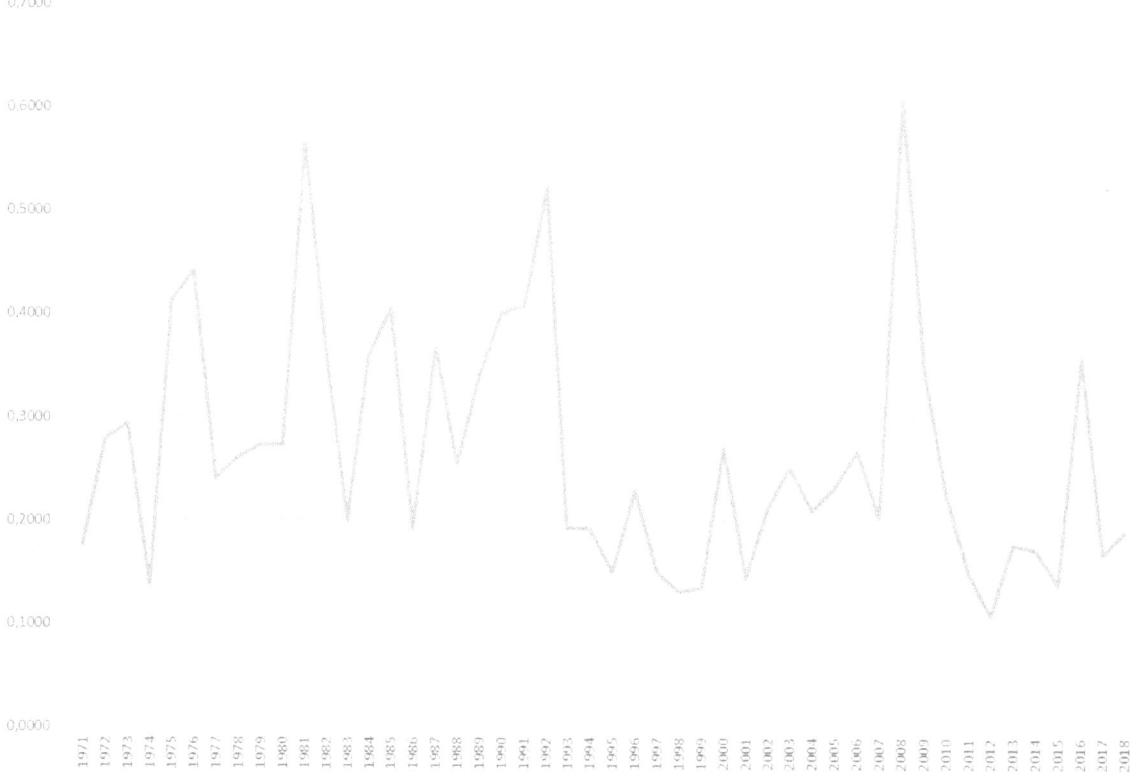

The highest portion of GDP in the UK comes from the service sector. For example, in the US it is financial services and technology sectors (Appendix 24)

Moreover, the London Stock Exchange is one of the oldest, largest and cover more than 60 countries, including Kazakhstan. In the financial sector, it is especially important that services are based on high quality, trust, and long-term relationships.

However, the service sector is also more speculative. And it requires some understanding of the world's demand for global currency, development, and progress. For example, Figure 7 also confirms that the UK currency is more volatile even though the EUR/USD market has more traders and investors.

This is also a point that in the future we will see more price volatility and in many indicators of the country.

Generally, for more research and analysis, you can check out historical data for GBP/USD (1971-2019) in Appendix 2.

JPY/USD

The third most popular in the world and most used Asian currency is the Japanese Yen, which is a currency of Japan.

It has also a long history, starting from the 8th century. But today, the Japanese Yen is one of the most popular, liquid and stable currencies.

You can notice it from the historical data in Figure 8.

Figure 8 Open and Close Rates for USD/JPY (1971 - 2019)

From Figure 8, we can see that the Japanese Yen was strengthening up until 2011. Generally, the economy of Japan was prospering and showing high stability and the currency was one of the main instruments to provide competitiveness of the country.

Today, Japan is one of the 4th largest economies in the world with GPD equal 4,97 trillion USD dollars in 2018.

We can notice from Figure 9 and 10 that USD/JPY has not extreme fluctuations between max and min levels.

One of the main reasons are:

1) Japanese economy strived to be one of the stable economies.
2) The economy accumulated special funds to keep the economy stable.

3) According to some experts, Japanese experts count 100 Yen as a 1 Unit currency of the country to regulate it and the economy effectively. And if you look at Figure 9, you can notice that 1 Unit of Japanese currency was fluctuating near 1 US dollar from 1990s.
4) Japan has the most advanced economy for research, innovation, and development, which keeps the economy stable.

Figure 9 Max and Min Rates for USD/JPY (1971 - 2018)

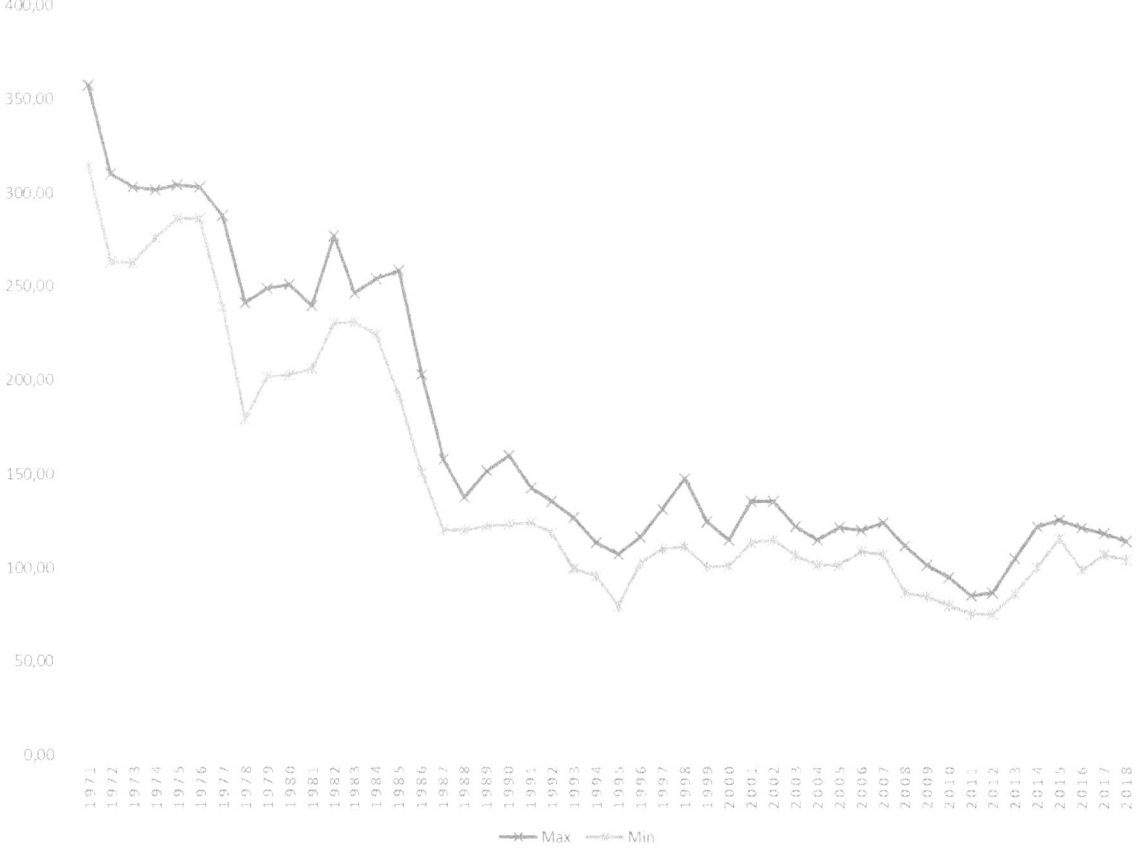

Figure 10 also supports the idea that the currency has a minimal difference between the max and min rates from the 1990s.

So, what to expect with Japanese currency and economy in the future?

Several years ago, I was participating in the Japanese Government Contest and writing about Japanese main barriers and opportunities in the future with the title of the essay: "The Leadership Role of Japanese Companies in the Global Trade and Development".

I outlined the following main areas of Japanese focus that time as follows:

1) Future industries;
2) Processes for integration and trade;
3) Content and search engines;
4) Mobility infrastructure;
5) Sustainable growth;

6) Additional and value-creating services.

For example, Japan has a very strong experience in technologies and many other areas. But till the moment, they are not accessible because of language barriers. One example, in Japan the content of the most web-sites are in Japanese language only.

Figure 10 Differences Between Max and Min Rates for USD/JPY (1971 - 2018)

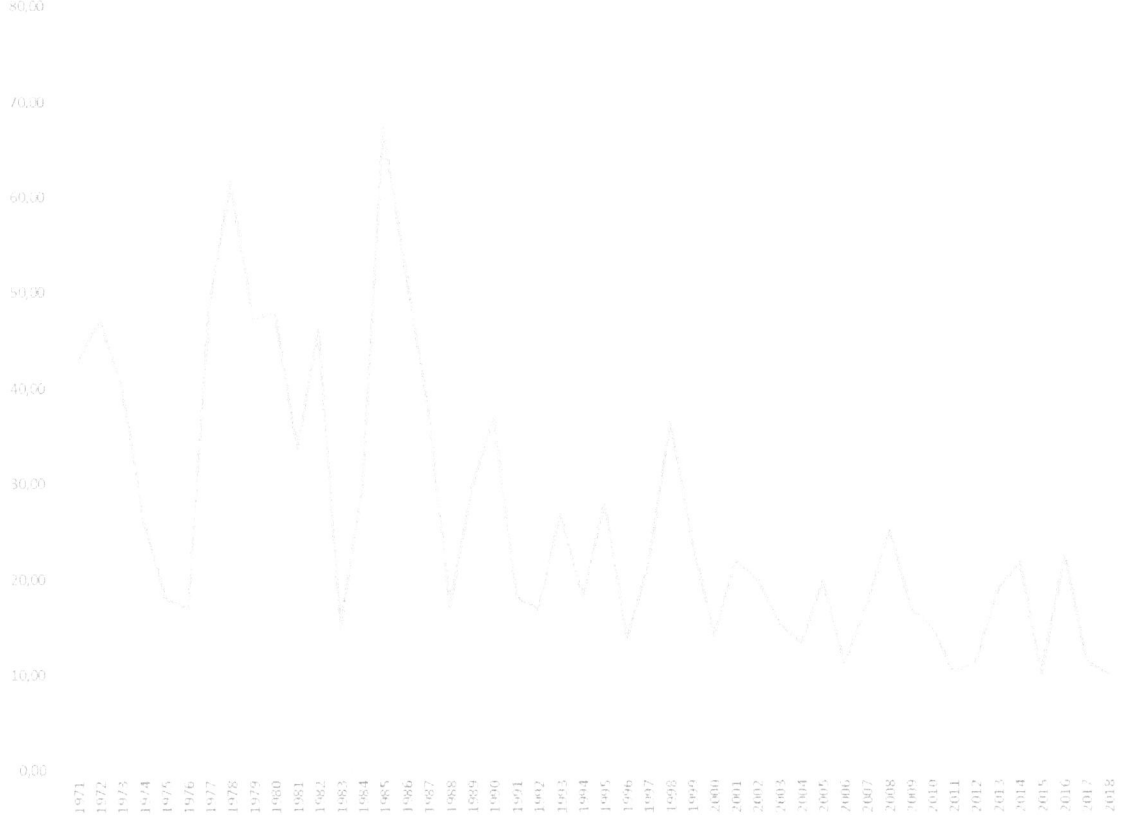

In addition, taking into account Japanese advanced infrastructure, industries, and high-qualified specialists, one can notice the global growth in the following five trade areas:

1) Industrial and commercial robots and computers.
2) Sustainable technologies, machines, cars, and products.
3) Sea service engineering and technologies.
4) Tourism for education, technology transfer, research, and cultural arts.
5) Mobility services and technologies.
6) Space navigation and control systems.

So, taking all this into account, the prediction for the Japanese economy is in strengthening the Yen. It will be not a dramatic change. But it will keep the economy stable to innovate the markets further.

You can find the historical data for USD/JPY (1971-2019) for additional research and forecast in Appendix 3.

XAU/USD

For centuries, gold was a premium asset for saving, controlling and politics. First global currencies such as USD, JPY, GBP were all linked to the gold in the past.

Widely used for jewelry, it also kept as a main saving asset. That's why gold was so valuable to invest, trade and save. With the development of new technologies and the availability of gold via online, demand for gold increased, especially from the beginning of 2000 (Figure 11).

Figure 11 Open and Close Prices for XAU/USD (1971 - 2019)

Summarizing the trends, the following factors can be reasons for gold demand:

1) The high volume of sales of jewelry.
2) Stability of the gold price as it limited in nature.
3) High demand for countries to keep it as a reserve.
4) The economic situation in the US, Europe, and other economies. The more stagnation in the economy, the higher the gold prices. As investors and traders prefer to invest and keep their assets in stable gold.
5) Alternative metals and currencies, such as cryptocurrencies can cause the price of gold down and make it very volatile.

Let's check figure 12. Even though the prices of gold went up, here, we can see that the volatility of rate is increased several times.

Figure 12 Max and Min Prices for XAU/USD (1971 - 2018)

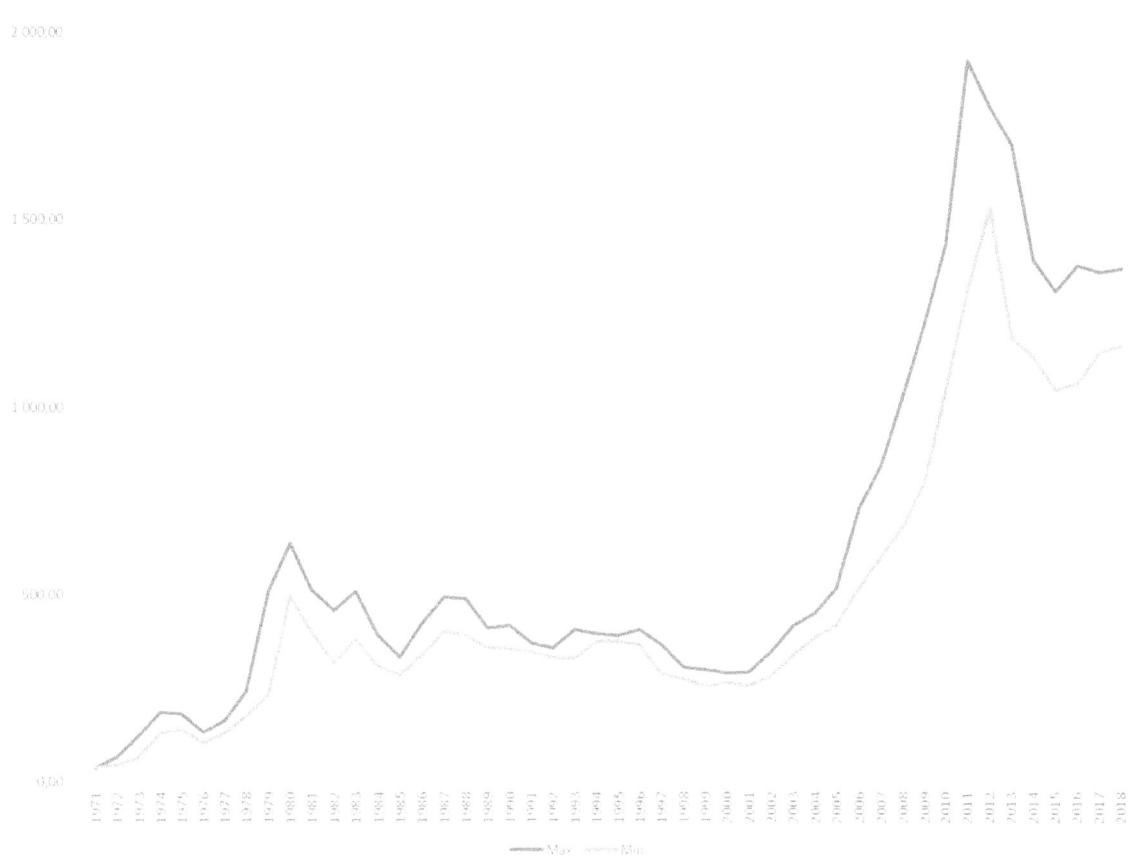

On the other hand, with the development of new technologies, we can see a lot of other new metals and precious stones, which are available as alternatives in the market.

Moreover, from 2012 we see the growth of electronic currencies, which provide better liquidity, opportunity to earn from the flow of electronic blocks and more transparency in operations.

Figure 12 shows the fading fluctuation of the differences between max and min prices for XAU/USD, starting from 2010. It also confirms that the gold prices will move down in the near future.

Generally, gold is trading in all major markets (Appendix 18) and in all time zones (Appendix 17).

At some point, gold becomes like an oil, which has a value, but at the same time, more and more people use alternative energy sources. With gold, it is cryptocurrencies, which gives more advantages for saving, trading and investing.

Again, because the United States is one of the largest economies and the US is the most stable currency, the gold is traded in US dollars.

However, it is important to mention, that Bitcoin Gold is now becoming popular and is one of the top 50 cryptocurrencies, with a market capitalization around 470 million US dollars (Appendix 19).

Figure 13 Differences Between Max and Min Prices for XAU/USD (1971 - 2018)

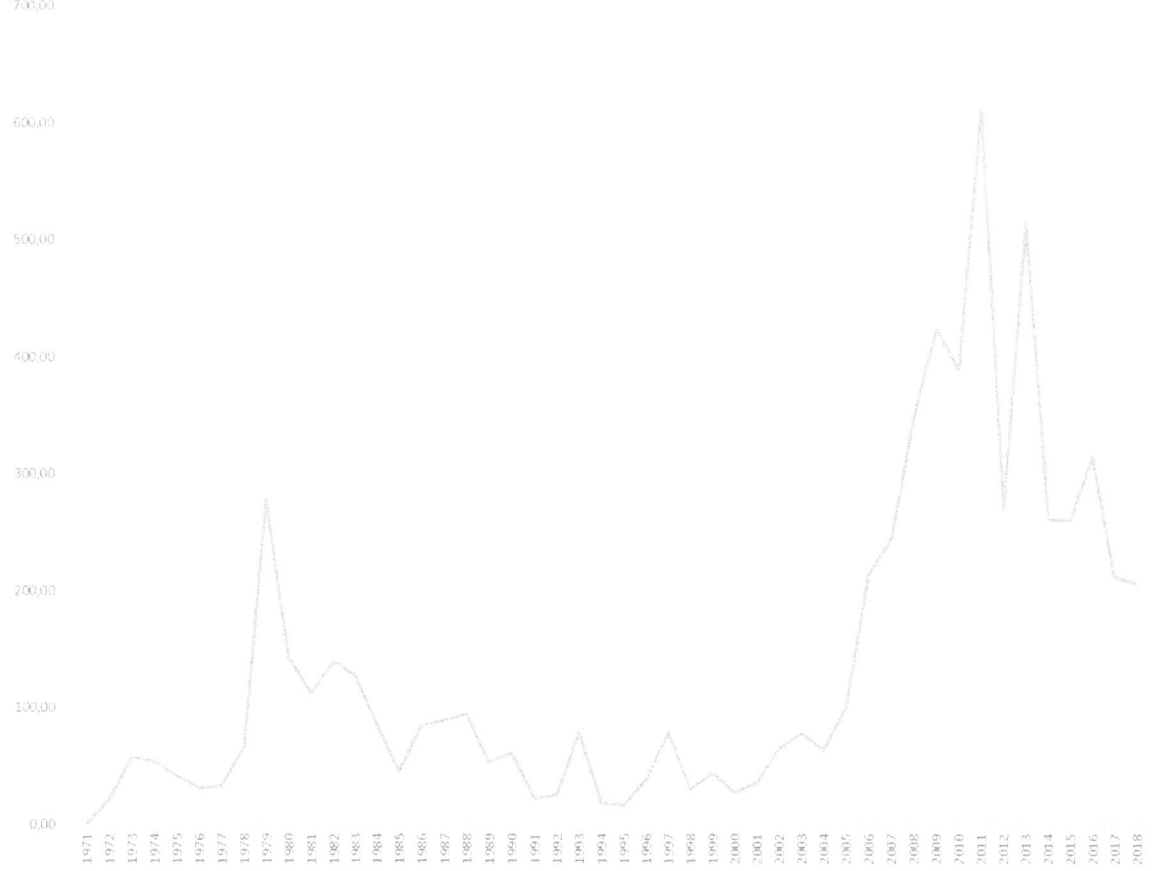

It shows that Gold is actively traded in cryptocurrency markets as well.

Generally, you can find historical data for XAU/USD (1971-2019) for additional research in Appendix 4.

Crude Oil WTI Futures

We have two types of barometers of oil. One is Brent and the other is WTI.

WTI stands for West Texas Intermediate (WTI) and it is an evaluation metric for crude oil used in oil pricing, which is defined in the New York Mercantile Exchange.

Previously, the WTI was traded close to Brent and OPEC basket, nowadays there are no interrelations of both barometers. For example, now Crude Oil WTI traded at 55,75 and Brent 62,84.

In Figure 14, you can check the Crude Oil WTI Future open and close prices for a period from 1994 to 2019.

Figure 14 Open and Close Prices for Crude Oil WTI Futures (1984 - 2019)

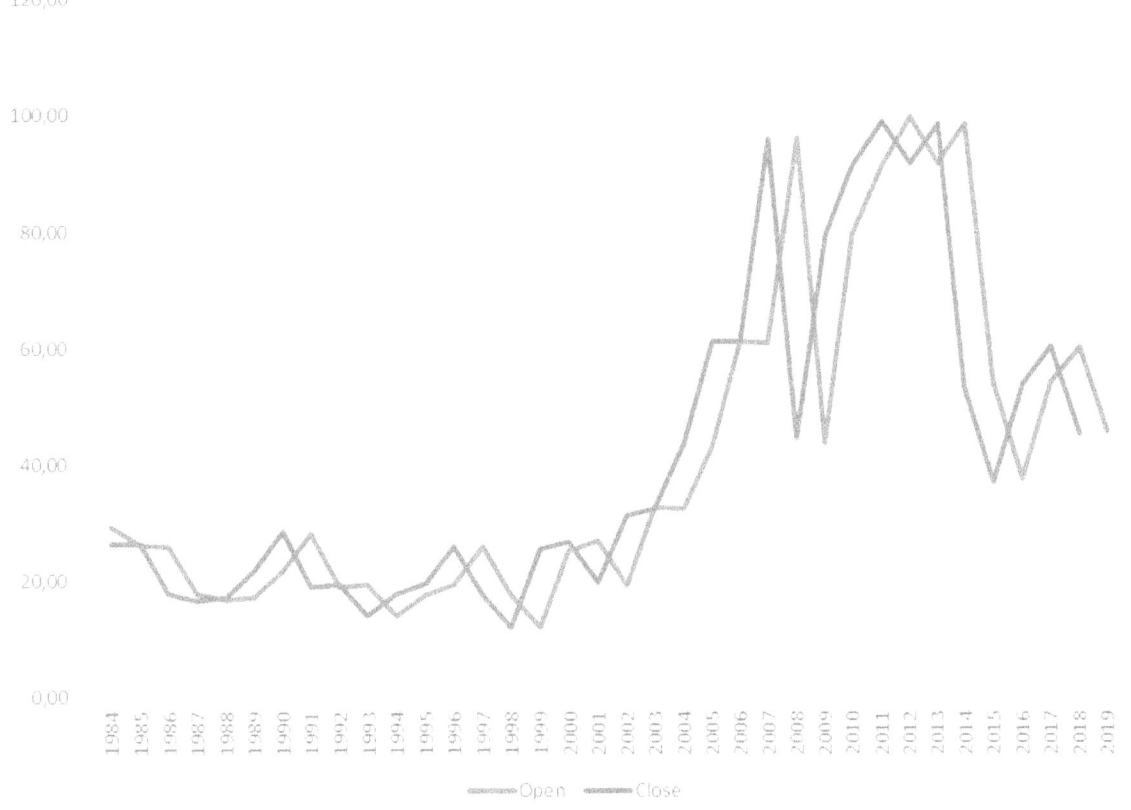

Figure 14 shows that the prices for Crude Oil WTI Futures fall into a downward trend and were highly volatile from 2005.

From Figure 15, analyzing the max and min prices, we can also see high volatility between max and min prices, starting from the year 2005.

The main factors for oil volatility are the following:

1) Sanctions. Some countries were under sanctions for many years. So, when countries revoked sanctions, the oil countries started to increase their supply.

2) Alternative sources of energy. Many countries are implementing alternative sources of energy for years. As a result, many European countries, which were the main consumption markets for oil are now using their own alternative energy sources.

3) Realization of green concepts. For example, in many countries, petrol cars are gradually replaced by electric cars and vehicles.

Figure 15 Max and Min Prices for Crude Oil WTI Futures (1984 - 2018)

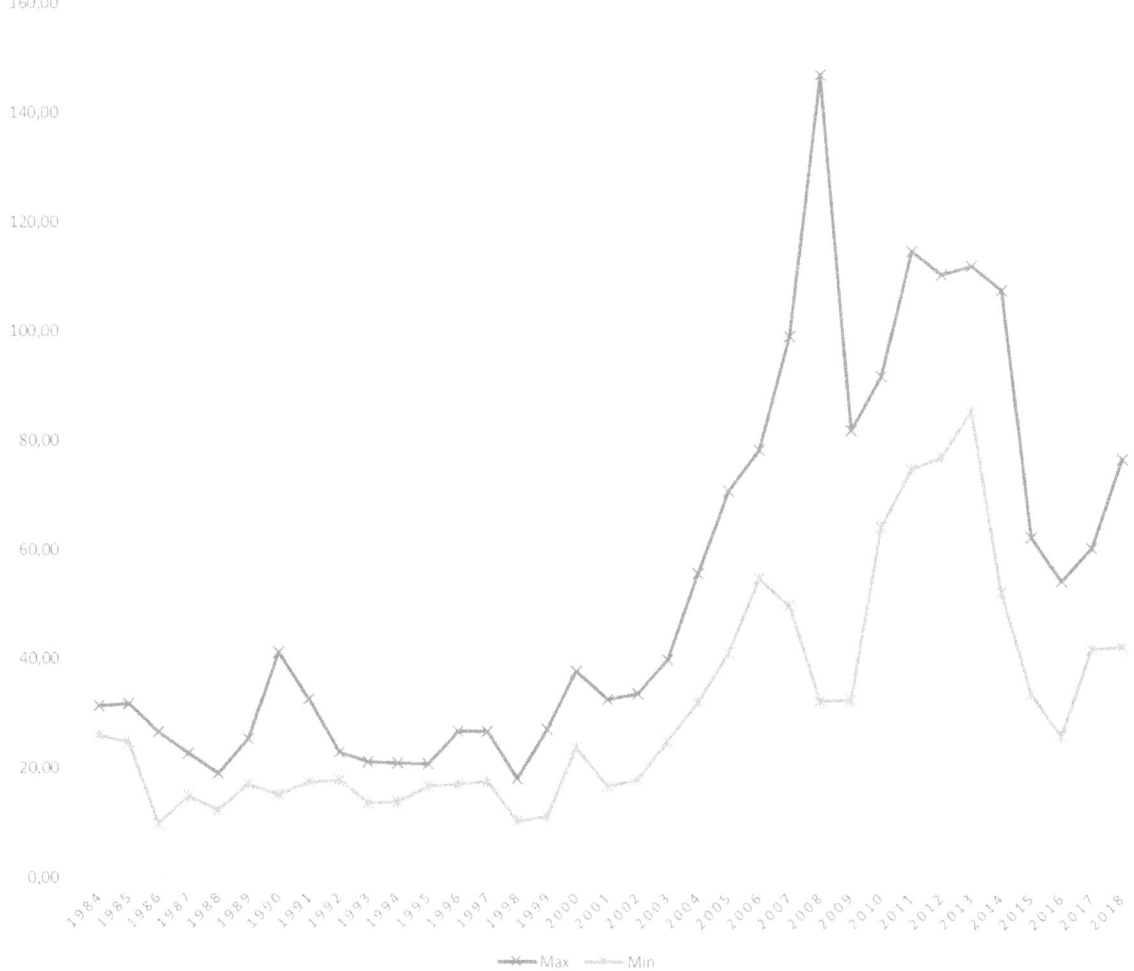

4) Technological advances. New innovative engines are now using less fuel or use them in combination with other patrols, for example, gas.

There is a question: where are the prices for oil heading?

If human beings will really learn how to progress in using electrical batteries and other sources of energy, the oil becomes unnecessary and very cheap. But at the same time, many poor countries or families will be interested to use it as a source of energy. And in this case, they will continue to use oil for many decades.

Another scenario, oil prices will go up quickly very soon as in many countries oil reserves will be finishing. It will soar the oil prices in the coming 20 years to more than

1000 US dollars per barrel, especially, in a period of high demand from developing countries.

Figure 16 Differences Between Max and Min Prices for Crude Oil WTI Futures (1984 - 2018)

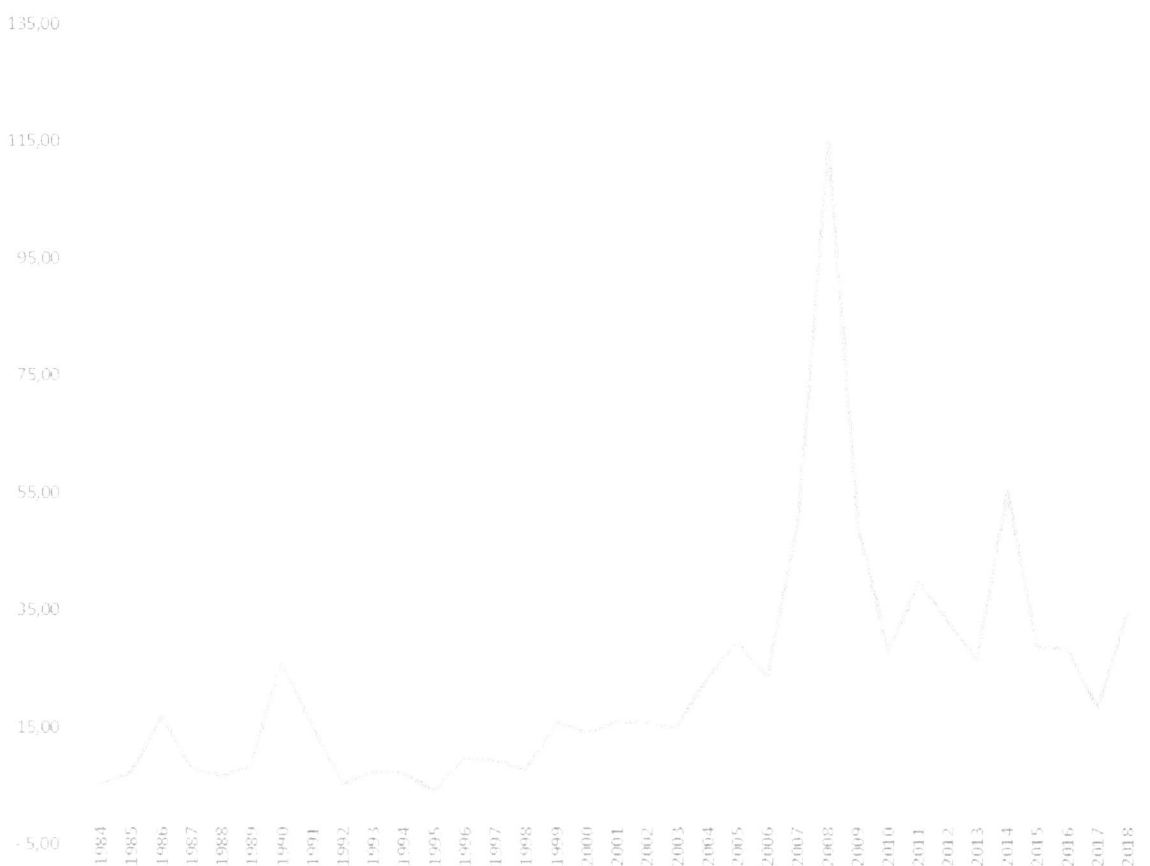

Figure 16 gives a tiny hope that oil prices will go up very soon. Because, if it will be expensive and scarce, many people think about alternative energy sources and definitely, for example, change their cars for electric ones as well.

In this case, many oil countries can benefit from high prices, but generally, the amount of consumption will be less hazardous for the planet.

Today, unlimited consumption of oil causes the following issues:

1) The era of automobiles. There are so many new, used and old cars because of cheap fuel on the roads.
2) The traffic. There is so huge traffic of airlines, cars, ships and trucks on the planet that they highly influence the Earth's ecology, economy, and future.
3) Pollution. The more oil used – the more the Earth becomes hot and polluted. There are also many cars on the planet from the 1980s.
4) The diseases. High level of pollution of air causes many breath, skin and heart problems. It also influences youth and future generations.

5) The wars. As consumption increased, we could saw many wars and social turmoil in different parts of the world in the last decades. Easy money from rigs attracts the best companies and at the same time - many robbers.

6) The problem of allocation of capital. In some countries, many funds are generated but the sums are allocated to a limited number of people. At the same time, these countries have social issues, a high level of poverty, economic and political issues.

7) Ecological catastrophes. Many oil and transport companies exploit their rigs and pipes without safety and environmental standards. And we can now see there are many oil spots on the land and water surfaces.

8) Climate change. According to many scientists and experts, automobiles are the main contributor to climate change on our planet. Melting of glaciers, record high temperatures, flooding, and hurricanes are those effects that we can hear and see nowadays as pieces of evidence.

There are indeed many harmful effects of oil consumption. And we have to gradually stop this issue forever to save a living environment for human beings.

So, the future forecast for oil is definitely ascending trend. It will help to stop consumption and use alternative technologies as well.

You can find historical data for Crude Oil WTI (1984-2019) in Appendix 5.

BTC/USD

Bitcoin is the latest, most used, liquid and popular cryptocurrency with capitalization around 190 billion USD dollars.

It is based on peer-to-peer and blockchain technology, which works without central banks, by managing payments and issuing bitcoins by the network itself.

This attracts many users and owners and from Figure 17, we can see a real picture of the value of the bitcoin

Bitcoin is open-source and public, so everyone can purchase it from any place around the world. Therefore, bitcoin became a disruptive new technology, which changes the global payment system.

Figure 17 Open and Close Rates for BTC/USD (2012 - 2019)

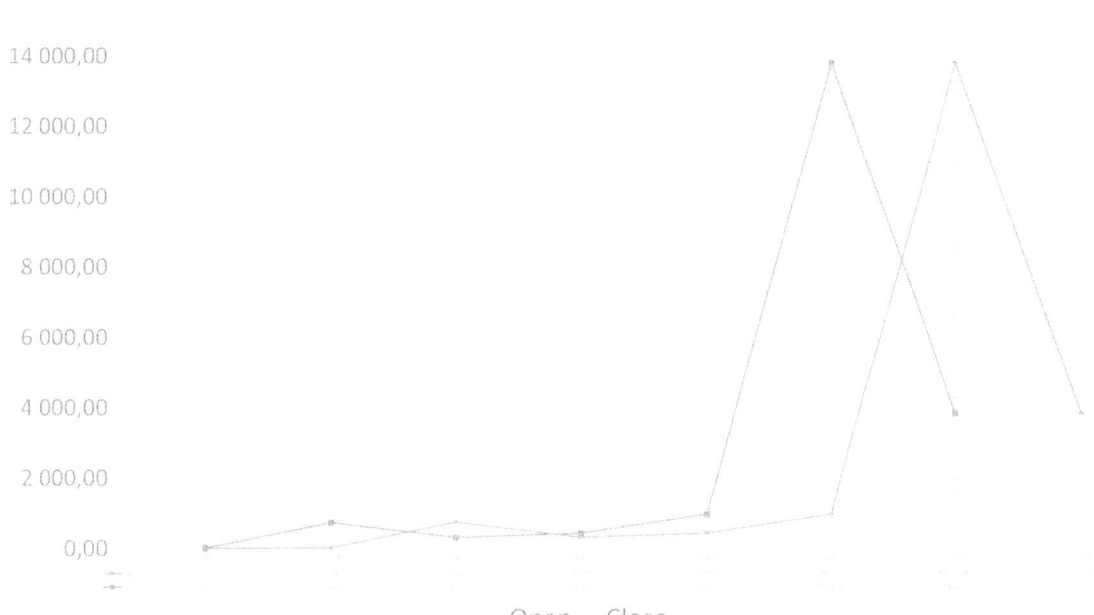

Figure 17 shows that the price of the bitcoin increased by more than 10 000 times in 2016. At the beginning of 2019, the rate for BTC/USD was around 4000 USD dollars, and now the rate for BTC/USD is around 10 000 US dollars per bitcoin (20 June 2019).

As an alternative currency, BTC is getting and becoming a real asset for investment, payments, and trade.

Why not oil or gold?

There are several reasons and let's count them:

1) Bitcoin is based on transparent technology;
2) Anyone can create a wallet free of charge;
3) Anyone can earn or buy bitcoin and trade at any time;

4) Anyone can invest and earn bitcoins by technologies available online.
5) Anyone can exchange it to many other assets.
6) In some countries, you can pay with bitcoin or other currencies.

With oil, gold and any other physical crops, you cannot do it.

However, from Figure 18 we can see that there are huge differences between max and min prices for BTC/USD. So, it shows a certain high level of risks as a currency.

Figure 18 Max and Min Rates for BTC/USD (2012 - 2018)

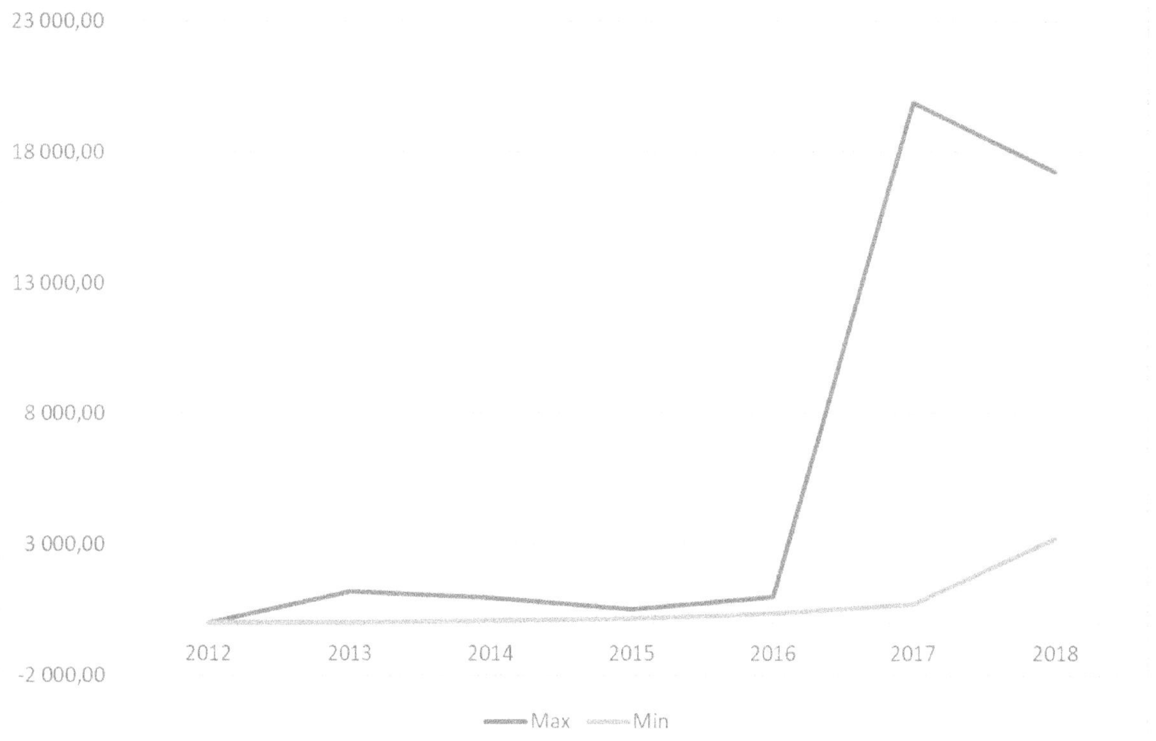

But it is normal for new products and technologies in any case.

The main point, with bitcoin humanity, can solve many issues, such as:

1) Lack of capital. Bitcoin if capitalized can be equal to 1 billion US dollar and easily solve the problem of capital insufficiency for many projects in the future.
2) Lack of transparency. There are many corrupted systems created in the world. Cryptocurrency technologies allow eliminating those corrupted networks because all transactions are transparent with Bitcoin technologies.
3) Political cases. In many countries, authoritarian governors persecute citizens and opponents for political reasons. They arrest bank accounts, businesses and do not let them go out of the country. The same situation happens in many soviet countries including Kazakhstan. The cryptocurrency infrastructure can be a real source of income and living against the unfairness from the government and its authoritarian regulations.
4) Lack of investment. Today, with bitcoin and more than 2000 cryptocurrencies, users try many projects of global importance. These projects are transparent,

can be easily evaluated for fakes, and are market sensitive. If the market is limited, the cryptocurrency can disappear very soon or can be replaced by the newest technology. If it is demanding, the market capitalization grows constantly.

Generally, bitcoin technology connects human activities with the digital world and activities. Without it, there is no future for the development of new technologies.

Even though one can see huge differences between max and min prices for BTC/USD in Figure 19, bitcoin and cryptocurrencies have a high level of interest from people and investors. There are now more than 2 000 cryptocurrencies. And capitalization of some of them is bigger than the GDP of several countries. You can check the top 50 cryptocurrencies in Appendix 19.

Figure 19 Differences Between Max and Min Rates for BTC/USD (2012 - 2018)

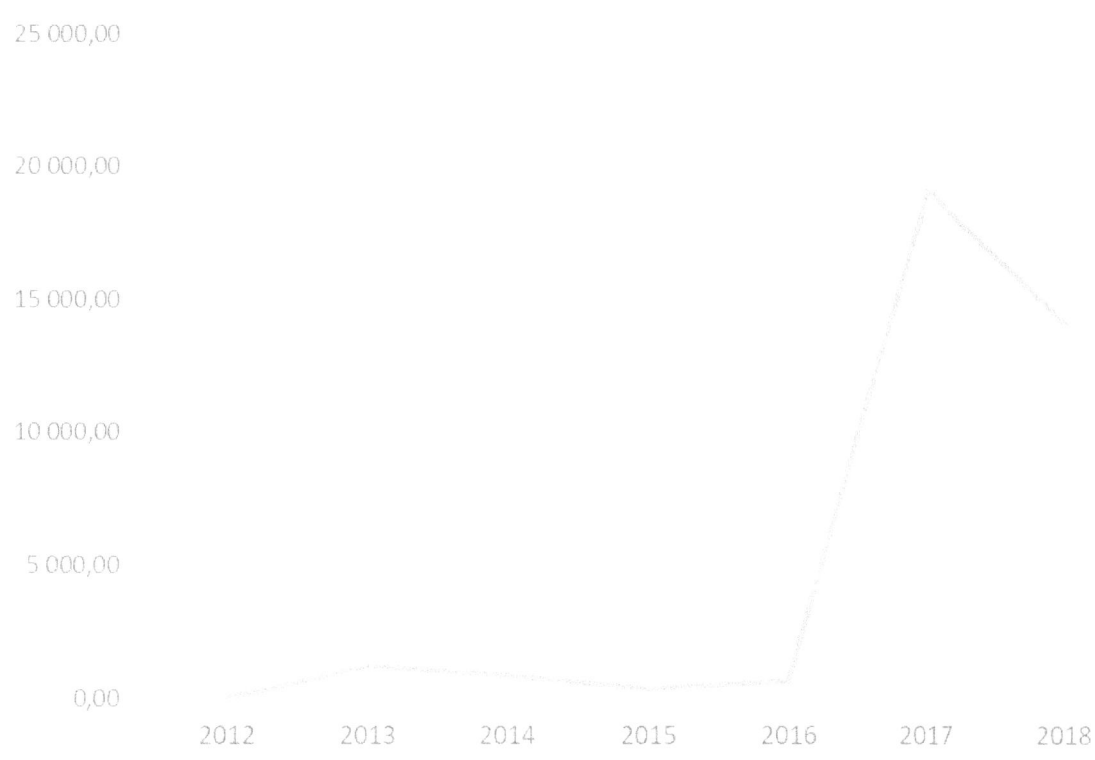

What will be the future forecast for BTC/USD?

As BTC replaces with its wallets, investment and trading possibilities all the present systems, it will b growing its capitalization. The same will be with other leading cryptocurrencies.

Cryptocurrencies such as Litecoin (LTC), TRON (TRX), Stellar (XML), Ripple (XRP), Bitcoin Cash (BCH), Cardano (ADA), Dogecoin (DOGE) will be among the most popular currencies to save and invest. For more please check the top 50 cryptocurrencies in Appendix 19.

The future will definitely bring us to the level when different payment cards will be created to pay with cryptocurrencies at any country. That time, the value of BTC/USD will be above 1 million US dollars per 1 BTC. And this future is not far from the horizon.

For more analysis, you can find historical data for BTC/USD (1912-2019) in Appendix 6.

S&P500

S&P500 is an American market index of the 500 active companies, which is calculated based on their capitalizations. The market capitalization of S&P500 is around 25 trillion US dollars and it is around 75-80% of the whole list of S&P companies. It is one of the most demanding for marketers, traders and investors to follow.

Figure 20, shows open and close indicators for S&P500 for a period from 1971 to 2019.

Figure 20 Open and Close Indicators for S&P500 (1971 - 2019)

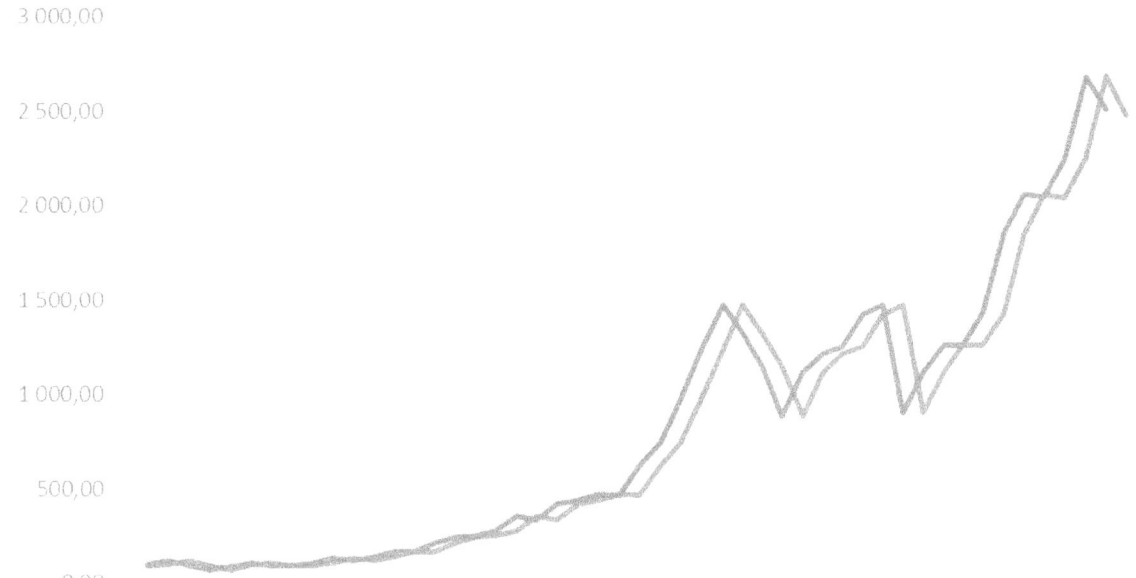

As you can see from Figure 20, it shows the smooth growing trend for 4 decades. At the same time, from 1989 to 2019 the market capitalization increased from 2,4 trillion US dollars to 24,4 trillion US dollars, i.e. 10 times.

This proves that US stocks of the 500 companies are attractive and profitable in the long-run.

It is clear that there are different kind of companies, successful and not so. But, the growth of index and market capitalization demonstrate that most of the companies increased in value more than 10 times. For example, the stock price of Amazon company increased more than 40 times (Appendix 20) or Apple stock prices – more than 265 times (Appendix 21).

It also shows that not all companies from the list of S&P500 are successful and for marketers, it gives a signal that fundamental analysis of stocks and companies are very important. Even though it is out of the topic of this book.

Figure 21 shows the max and min indicators for S&P500 for a period from 1971 to 2018. And generally, the graph shows growing differences between annual max and min levels (Figure 22).

Figure 21 Max and Min Indicators for S&P500 (1971 - 2018)

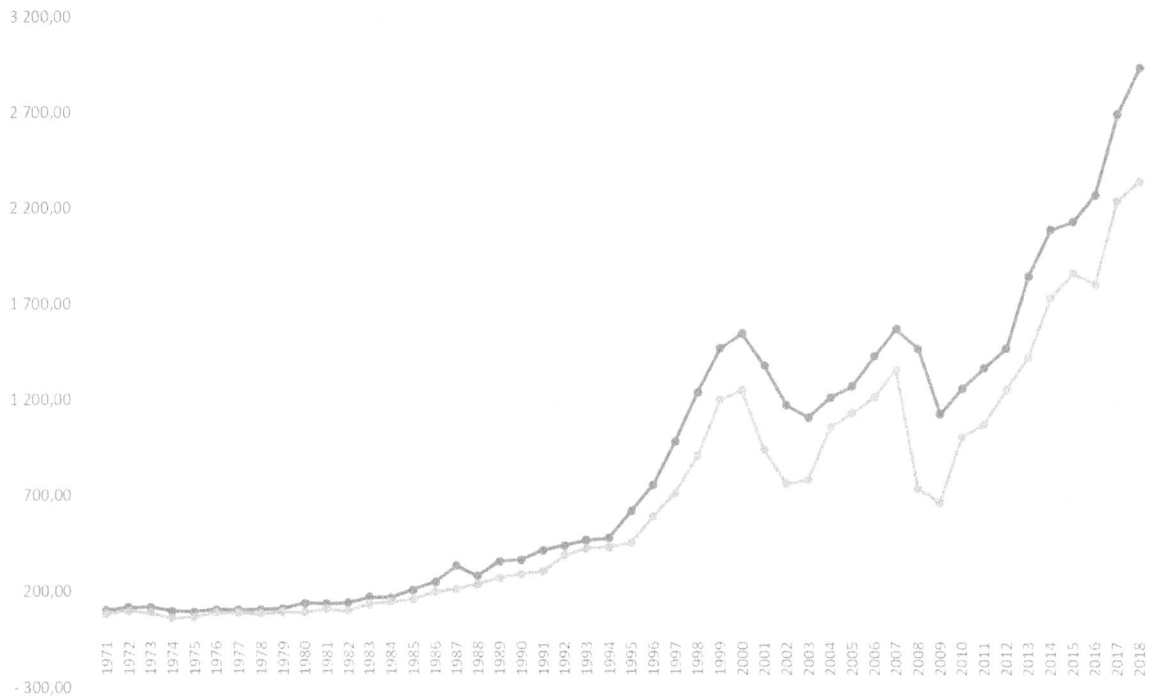

From Figure 21 we can see two bottoms and 2 peak levels and the third one is still heading toward new heights.

This is proved also from Figure 22, which shows a steady increase in differences between annual max and min levels.

However, the general index for 500 companies has many risks. Therefore, even we can see high growth of some leading companies, we can see high fluctuations of the general index.

No matter of this fact, the trend will continue to grow further. At some point, it will go down but the US economy and its innovative companies will help to quickly recover the index and move it ascending. To illustrate, according to Investing.com, the average growth rate of S&P500 is around 9,38%.

But depending on selected stocks, your portfolio can show better results. For example, my portfolio on Investopedia Simulator of 12 stocks from the list of S&P500 companies has showed at least 50% of growth in 3 years, with average annual return rate around 16% (Appendix 25).

The selection of the best stocks requires the following:

1) Analysis of companies, its history, and its results;
2) Industry analysis;

3) Management analysis;
4) Patent and innovation analysis.
5) Country analysis.

The constant analysis helps to find out the necessary information about the future perspectives of the company and its stocks. So, you will make the right decision on investment.

Figure 22 Differences Between Max and Min Indicators for S&P500 (1971 - 2018)

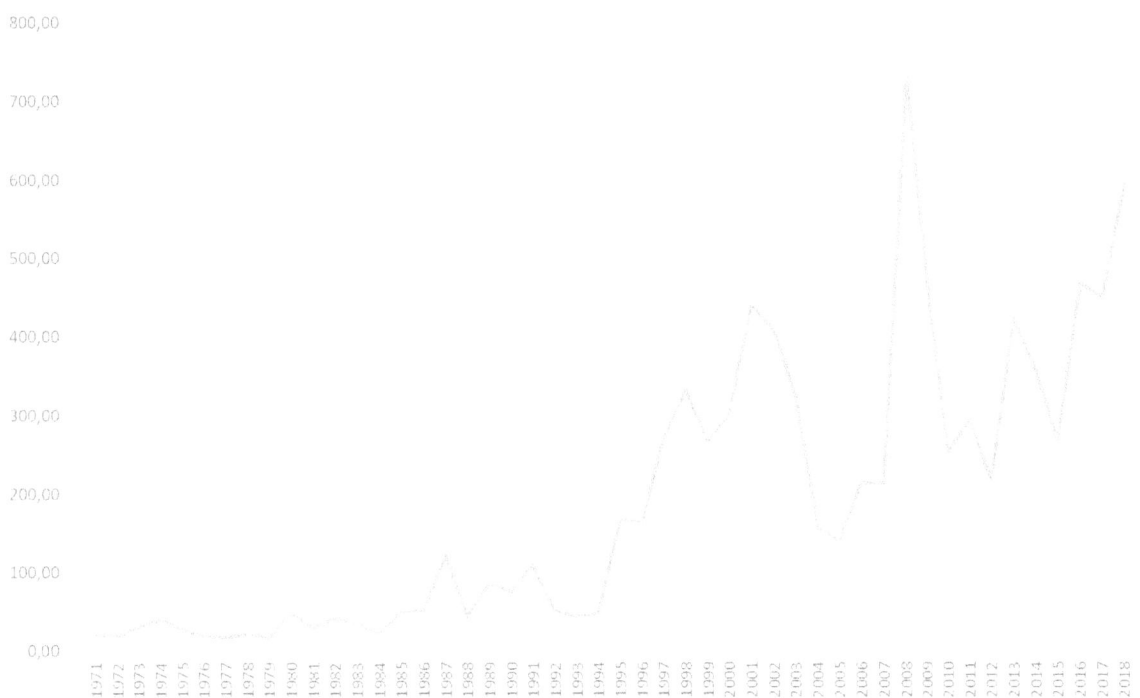

For further analysis of the list of S&P500 companies, you can check out Appendix 22.

For additional analysis of historical data of S&P500 (1971-2019), you can review the Appendix 7.

FTSE100

FTSE100 is The Financial Times Stock Exchange 100 Index, which is an index of 100 largest companies, selected by the Financial Times from the London Stock Exchange. The FTSE is calculated similarly to the S&P500 based on all the market capitalizations of all stocks and divided by the divisor. The total market capitalization of FTSE100 is about 2 trillion GB pounds. It is about 10 times less than S&P500.

In Figure 23 below, you can see a historical chart for open and close indicators of the FTSE100 for a period from 2002 to 2019.

Figure 23 Open and Close Indicators for FTSE100 (2002 - 2019)

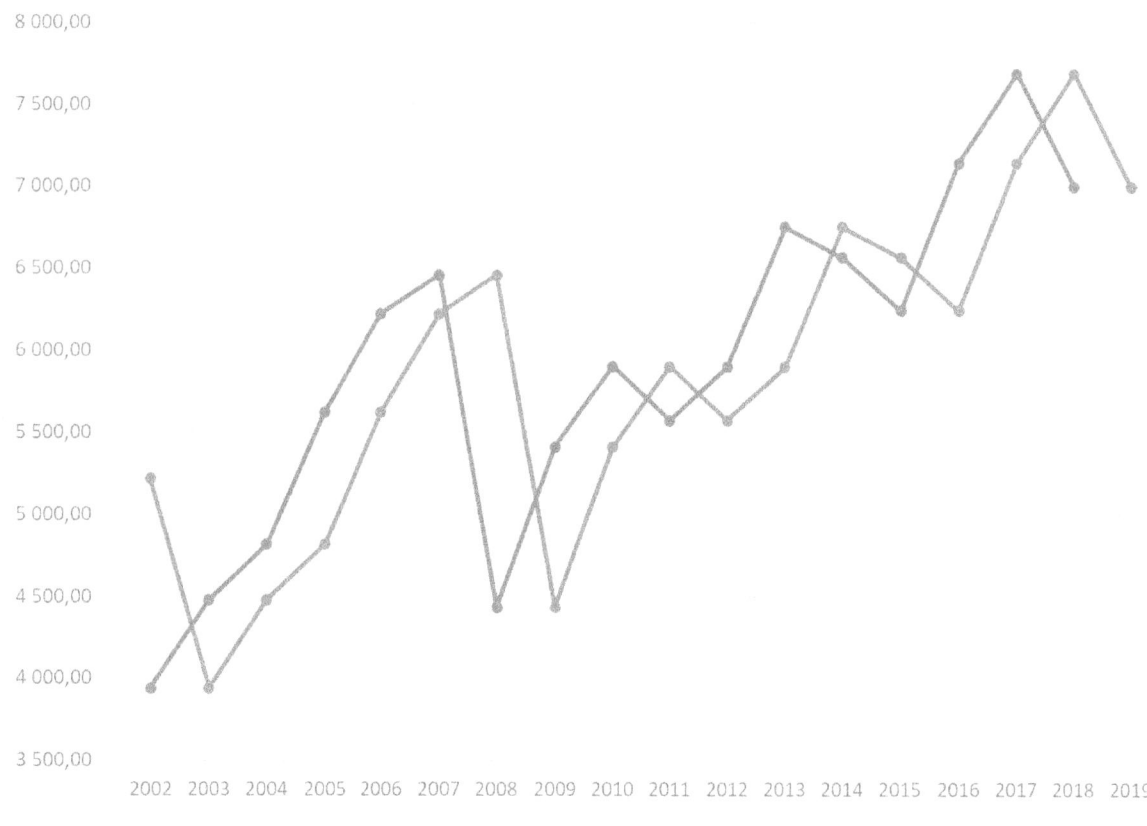

Generally, from the above Figure, one can see the ascending trend of the FTSE100 index. And it also shows the profitability of the stocks of the London Stock Exchange in the long-run. Therefore, it is attractive for investors to invest and trade.

From Figure 24, we can see the annual max and min levels of the FTSE100. And it shows that it is quite attractive for short and mid-term traders and investors.

Generally, Figure 24 shows a steady growth of the index, which means that FTSE companies are dynamic and stable.

However, despite the fact that the index had a negative sign of -7 for the year 2018, the annualized growth rate if calculated, for example for 10 or 20 years, will show annual growth of 3-4%.

Based on gradual growth and taking into account that the UK is one of the innovative countries, the FTSE100 will steadily grow in the future.

Figure 24 Max and Min Indicators for FTSE100 (2002 - 2018)

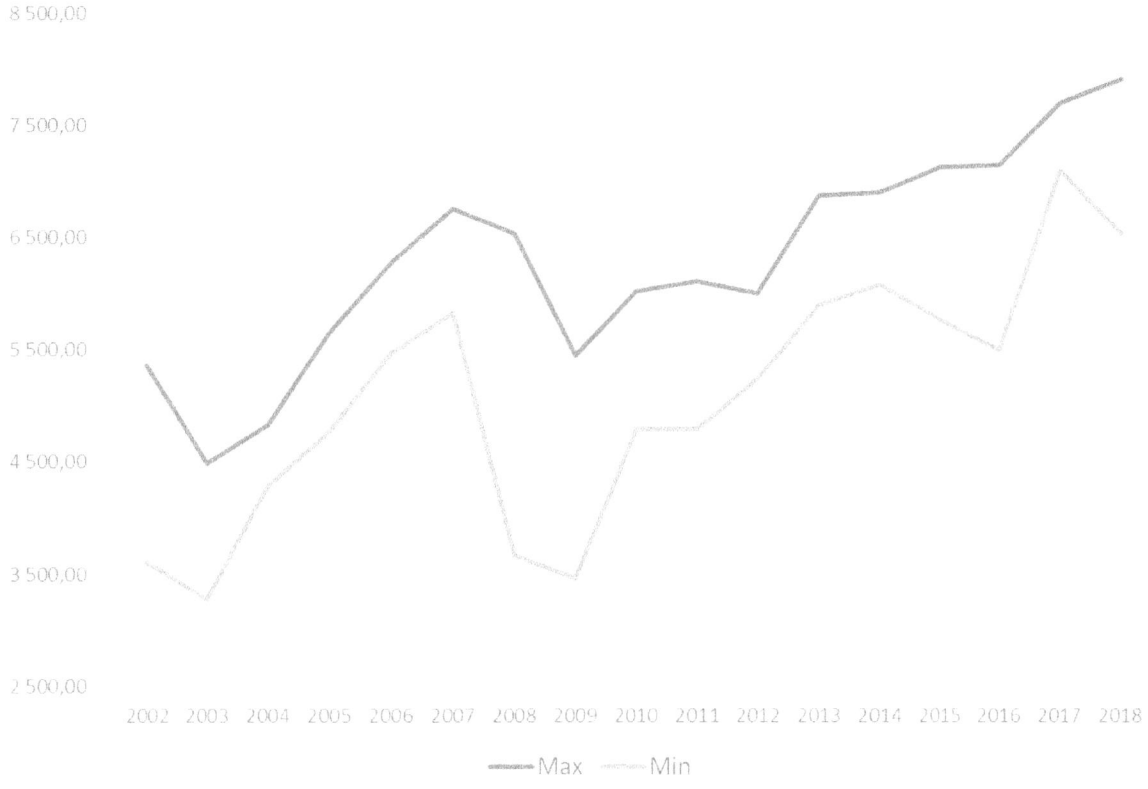

Differences of the max and min levels prove also that the index is more or less stable (Figure 25).

One of the main reasons for the stable growth of the FTSE100 is the following:

1) The UK is the number 4 economy of the world;
2) London Stock Exchange is the largest Stock Exchange in Europe and the Eurasian continent;
3) The UK is one of the largest financial centers in the world.
4) London and generally the UK is one of the oldest educational and research centers of the world;
5) Bank of England is one of the oldest central banks of the world;
6) London is the largest trade hub for bonds, futures, stocks, currencies, and insurances;
7) London is the head office of the major global and international banks etc.

All these factors make London and the UK the most attractive places for professionals. For sure, it provides the economy with stability, high income, and new innovations.

However, let's check what can cause negative effects for the FTSE100 and in turn to the economy of the UK and London. The following are the most important issues:

1) Brexit;
2) Migration policy;
3) Climate Change;
4) Development of competitive financial centers in Europe.

Therefore, it is important to do constant monitoring of historical data to see how markets are changing and why they are changing.

Figure 25 Differences Between Max and Min Indicators for FTSE100 (2002 - 2018)

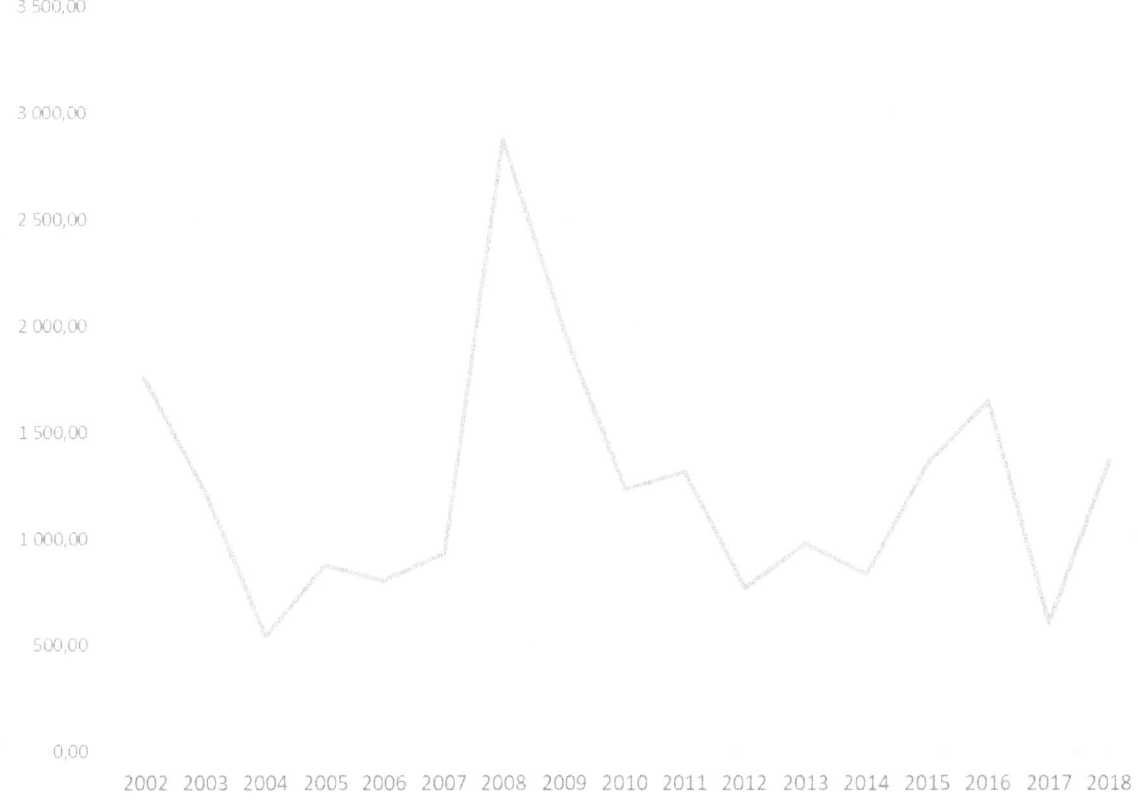

Like in S&P500, in the list of FTSE100, there are many companies which show the highest growth rate and there are a lot of laggards. So, fundamental company analysis is very important.

A list of FTSE100 companies you can find in Appendix 23 for your portfolio analysis.

For additional analysis of the historical data of FTSE100 (2002-2019), you can check the Appendix 8.

Asset Portfolio

Asset Portfolio Management is one of the main areas where knowledge about market trends can be a useful asset for your future.

Every investor or trader pays close attention to the asset portfolio. The more assets in your portfolio, the better the portfolio is defended from various risks.

For example, in Appendix 25, you can check my stock portfolio on Investopedia Simulator. It was opened in 2016 with 1 million virtual US dollar cash. And now you can see the asset's value is 1,61 million US dollars. The annual average growth is around 16%.

While selecting the assets, it is important to diversify your portfolio not only with stocks, but also currencies and other equities.

Why is it important?

As you can see in Appendix 25, assets are showing various outcomes in terms of growth. The best outcome is from EBIX stock, which shows more than 168% of growth. The worst outcome is from CABOT OIL&GAS CORPORATION, which shows -18% of the loss.

A total number of stocks in the portfolio is 12 stocks. They have various levels of outcomes. However, a common outcome is an annual growth rate, which is around 16% as we mentioned.

Great! This is the way, how the portfolio is managed effectively.

Before selecting your portfolio's assets, you have to do the following:

1) Analyze stocks, especially historical data;
2) Analyze stock prices in charts.
3) Analyze industry news and developments.
4) Analyze industry indices and graphs.
5) Understand major trends in industries and in the economy.
6) Compare the stocks.
7) Select your stocks for your portfolio.
8) Keep them in your portfolio to see the results.

The same procedure is for any asset.

However, with currencies, CFD and other trade options, you can trade in both directions, depending on the directions of the trends.

Today, for any marketer or investor, there are many options to include in the portfolio. For example, you can add to your portfolio the following assets:

1) Stocks or other equities;
2) CFD;
3) Commodities;

4) Currencies;
5) Cryptocurrencies;
6) Property;
7) Land;
8) Other assets.

Stock and other equities are customer sensitive, i.e. market sensitive, therefore they are profitable in the long-run.

Currencies depend on economic indicators and take time to take profit. Cryptocurrencies are a new trend. It helps users not only save money in the wallet but also invest and trade.

Property prices depend on the demographic situation in the country and in economies with decreasing demographic rates, it is difficult to make a profit. However, the property will not lose its value.

Commodity prices are climate-sensitive and seasonal. It is sometimes too risky to invest. You have to know well the commodity to decide on it and earn on trends.

The most stable growth rate is with the land. It increases in value, especially in the most densely populated regions. But it is not a liquid and attractive asset anymore.

Generally, you have to understand well your asset. And in this book, the purpose was to show the first steps to create your portfolio assets.

Final Outcome

The ultimate outcome of any market research and analysis over trends is a forecast, real improvement of the product, company, processes or market leadership.

In Table 7, we can compare these ultimate outcomes and see the real importance of the book for readers and users.

Table 7 Final Outcomes

	Forecast	**Improvement**	**Leadership**
Purpose	To predict the future and trends	To improve the condition or state of the product, company, process, etc.	To become a leader in the market
Dependent	Professional analytical model and forecast	Professional staff to improve	Professional staff
Benefit	Researcher, Company, Portfolio	Customers	Customer and Company
Costs	Low	High	Low to High
Actions	The calculation, Investment, Trading	Technical or Handwork	Management
Risk	Low to High	Medium-High	Medium-High
Strategy	Invest in the most profitable and demanding	Improve the quality of product or service to meet customer needs	Lead the market
Effects	From Short-term to Long-term	From Mid-term to Long-term	Mid-term and Long-term
Results	Profitability, Market share	Customers, Innovation, Profitability, Quality	Market share, Control, Innovation, Quality

From Table 7 we can see that market research and analysis over trends benefit in 3 main ways with different level of requirements, actions, and results. For example, by effective forecasting, an investor can increase profitability or market share of the company or portfolio. And, if the analysis was done appropriately, it will be a low-risk investment.

However, in a real situation, the outcome of the market research and analysis over trends depends on many other factors such as:

1) Availability of resources;
2) Leadership role;
3) Media coverage and PR;
4) Teamwork;

5) Technical competences;
6) Technology and equipment etc.;

To illustrate, after your forecast evaluation, you have to decide on investment or not and you have to make a decision how and with whom to start your actions. It is the topic, which is out of this book. However, it is important to understand that the main steps to realize the forecasts are your actions.

The same with improvements and leadership goals. You have to have a team, budget and clear goals what and how to do.

And you have to understand that analyzing markets and defining trends do not provide the final outcome. It only shows you the right information and the direction of where to go.

The final outcome is always your profitability and your achievements. Therefore, it requires a lot of work to do and questions to ask yourself.

Ask yourself

After reading this book and learning some new ideas, you will be easy on deciding to invest or trade, but do not hurry.

Stop for a while, analyze yourself and the market trends, ask yourself the following questions:

1) Have I learned to define markets trends?
2) Do I have the right skills and competences to invest and trade in the markets?
3) Am I ready to trade or invest in markets trends?
4) Do I have management skills to run my portfolio or project?
5) Do I have my team to realize my goals or projects?
6) Where am I the best at to use the advantages of a trend?
7) How to benefit from a market trend?
8) Do I have the capital to invest?
9) How to start my investment portfolio analysis? And who can help me?
10) What are the main platforms to invest and trade?
11) What are the best experts in market trends, investment, and trade?
12) What are the market rules I have to practice and follow every day?
13) Are there any new policies that I should to understand and learn about markets, market trends?

You have to answer many questions like above, long before you start your actions. And it is really about planning, acting and achieving your goals and plans. This is out of the topic and right now I can only provide you with the additional useful links below.

List of Web-sites

Here, you can find useful links to use the knowledge about the trends in the best way to benefit. You can try investing or trading or you can also try to come up with your own project to realize.

Feel free to contact me if you cannot find your useful link.

1) Investing.com. This web-site was one of the main sources of open and close prices for various markets
2) Investopedia.com. This web-site was one of the main sources of portfolio analysis.
3) Yahoo Finance: www.finance.yahoo.com
4) Market Watch: www.marketwatch.com
5) Blockchain wallet: www.blockchain.com
6) Coinbase wallet: www.coinbase.com
7) Binance Crypto Exchange: www.binance.com
8) Slickcharts: www.slickcharts.com
9) LSE Market Capitalization: www.lsemarketcap.com
10) Project Manager: https://www.projectmanager.com/training/make-action-plan
11) Trello Project Management: https://trello.com/
12) Teamweek: https://teamweek.com/

Please note, that all useful links presented here are suggestions only. There is no intention to advertise or offer them for working.

Conclusion

This book is my first book to explain market trends.

Being a marketing specialist and observing many markets every day you start to understand that every year is unique with its own trends.

You also understand that there are rules that make markets standard, repetitive or trendy.

Generally, it is vital to know the market trends in order to succeed in the market conditions. And this book was one of the first steps by which I started to disclose my unique experiences and information about the markets and trends.

I very hope that it will benefit all readers as a reference book and a tool for learning market trends.

I will be happy to see your comments and ideas about how I can improve my next editions of the book. I also welcome any think tank projects, where I can participate and contribute to resolving important issues of today's market economies.

Feel free send me your message or your comment via email at nurbek2002@yahoo.com

About author

Nigel Aksel is an individual investor and trader with more than 10 years of experience in research of markets, companies and investment portfolios. He is involved as a lecturer of marketing and management at the South-Kazakhstan State University.

Nigel enjoys writing about multiple issues of the investment, trade and other related topics. As a member of various institutions, he understands well about the problems of global investments, trade, and development. He explores many areas of the economy on how to make investments more effective and profitable in various markets.

Appendix

Appendix 1 Historical Data for EUR/USD (1975 – 2019)

Year	Open	Close	Difference (C-O)	Max	Min	Difference	Medium
1975	1,3446	1,2217	-0,1229	1,3835	1,2229	0,1606	1,3032
1976	1,2217	1,1952	-0,0265	1,2217	1,1707	0,051	1,1962
1977	1,1952	1,2833	0,0881	1,2891	1,1991	0,09	1,2441
1978	1,2833	1,4109	0,1276	1,5085	1,2863	0,2222	1,3974
1979	1,4109	1,4923	0,0814	1,5041	1,3849	0,1192	1,4445
1980	1,4923	1,2324	-0,2599	1,4923	1,3246	0,1677	1,4085
1981	1,2324	1,0708	-0,1616	1,2324	1,0378	0,1946	1,1351
1982	1,0708	0,9442	-0,1266	1,0708	0,9166	0,1542	0,9937
1983	0,9442	0,7914	-0,1528	0,9442	0,8201	0,1241	0,8822
1984	0,7914	0,7062	-0,0852	0,8561	0,7078	0,1483	0,7820
1985	0,7062	0,9062	0,2000	0,8887	0,6674	0,2213	0,7781
1986	0,9086	1,1244	0,2158	1,0701	0,9086	0,1615	0,9894
1987	1,1244	1,2243	0,0999	1,3084	1,0648	0,2436	1,1866
1988	1,2243	1,1098	-0,1145	1,3102	1,0805	0,2297	1,1954
1989	1,1098	1,2077	0,0979	1,2021	1,0095	0,1926	1,1058
1990	1,2077	1,3909	0,1832	1,4016	1,1684	0,2332	1,2850
1991	1,3909	1,2668	-0,1241	1,4189	1,1135	0,3054	1,2662
1992	1,2668	1,2023	-0,0645	1,4566	1,2011	0,2555	1,3289
1993	1,2023	1,1098	-0,0925	1,2484	1,0779	0,1705	1,1632
1994	1,1098	1,2248	0,1150	1,2813	1,0975	0,1838	1,1894
1995	1,2248	1,2751	0,0503	1,3521	1,2115	0,1406	1,2818
1996	1,2751	1,251	-0,0241	1,2968	1,2162	0,0806	1,2565
1997	1,2510	1,0947	-0,1563	1,2561	1,0396	0,2165	1,1479
1998	1,0947	1,1728	0,0781	1,2301	1,0662	0,1639	1,1482
1999	1,1728	1,0037	-0,1691	1,1899	0,9959	0,194	1,0929
2000	1,0037	0,941	-0,0627	1,0407	0,8202	0,2205	0,9305
2001	0,9410	0,8878	-0,0532	0,9576	0,8313	0,1263	0,8945
2002	0,8878	1,0454	0,1576	1,0505	0,8518	0,1987	0,9512
2003	1,0454	1,2554	0,21	1,2657	1,0301	0,2356	1,1479
2004	1,2554	1,3527	0,0973	1,3694	1,1731	0,1963	1,2713
2005	1,3527	1,1811	-0,1716	1,3575	1,1611	0,1964	1,2593
2006	1,1811	1,3178	0,1367	1,3368	1,1767	0,1601	1,2568
2007	1,3178	1,4562	0,1384	1,4969	1,2822	0,2147	1,3896
2008	1,4562	1,3962	-0,06	1,6038	1,2284	0,3754	1,4161
2009	1,3962	1,4314	0,0352	1,5141	1,243	0,2711	1,3786
2010	1,4314	1,3348	-0,0966	1,4584	1,184	0,2744	1,3212
2011	1,3348	1,2925	-0,0423	1,4938	1,2845	0,2093	1,3892
2012	1,2925	1,3183	0,0258	1,3486	1,2017	0,1469	1,2752
2013	1,3183	1,3723	0,054	1,3901	1,2708	0,1193	1,3305
2014	1,3723	1,2072	-0,1651	1,4001	1,2072	0,1929	1,3037
2015	1,2072	1,0848	-0,1224	1,2072	1,042	0,1652	1,1246
2016	1,0862	1,0516	-0,0346	1,1617	1,0353	0,1264	1,0985
2017	1,0532	1,1998	0,1466	1,2094	1,0494	0,16	1,1294
2018	1,2002	1,147	-0,0532	1,2556	1,1215	0,1341	1,1886
2019	1,1466						

Appendix 2 Historical Data for GBP/USD (1971 – 2019)

Year	Open	Close	Difference (C-O)	Max	Min	Difference	Medium
1971	2,4138	2,5878	0,1740	2,5878	2,4110	0,1768	2,4994
1972	2,5878	2,3772	-0,2106	2,6141	2,3351	0,2790	2,4746
1973	2,3772	2,2836	-0,0936	2,5778	2,2836	0,2942	2,4307
1974	2,2836	2,3772	0,0936	2,4211	2,2836	0,1375	2,3524
1975	2,3772	2,0236	-0,3536	2,4250	2,0124	0,4126	2,2187
1976	2,0236	1,7104	-0,3132	2,0249	1,5830	0,4419	1,8040
1977	1,7104	1,9490	0,2386	1,9490	1,7089	0,2401	1,8290
1978	1,9490	1,9893	0,0403	2,0843	1,8223	0,2620	1,9533
1979	1,9893	2,2629	0,2736	2,2629	1,9893	0,2736	2,1261
1980	2,2629	2,3719	0,1090	2,4345	2,1609	0,2736	2,2977
1981	2,3719	1,8719	-0,5000	2,3719	1,8063	0,5656	2,0891
1982	1,8719	1,5146	-0,3573	1,8719	1,5146	0,3573	1,6933
1983	1,5146	1,3968	-0,1178	1,5967	1,3968	0,1999	1,4968
1984	1,3968	1,1267	-0,2701	1,4856	1,1267	0,3589	1,3062
1985	1,1267	1,4055	0,2788	1,4839	1,0787	0,4052	1,2813
1986	1,4055	1,4774	0,0719	1,5560	1,3646	0,1914	1,4603
1987	1,4774	1,8833	0,4059	1,8304	1,4630	0,3674	1,6467
1988	1,8833	1,8064	-0,0769	1,9025	1,6479	0,2546	1,7752
1989	1,8064	1,6071	-0,1993	1,8280	1,4870	0,3410	1,6575
1990	1,6071	1,9318	0,3247	1,9865	1,5855	0,4010	1,7860
1991	1,9318	1,8691	-0,0627	2,0042	1,5966	0,4076	1,8004
1992	1,8691	1,5083	-0,3608	2,0124	1,4901	0,5223	1,7513
1993	1,5083	1,4753	-0,0330	1,5972	1,4045	0,1927	1,5009
1994	1,4753	1,5643	0,0890	1,6450	1,4523	0,1927	1,5487
1995	1,5643	1,5462	-0,0181	1,6681	1,5182	0,1499	1,5932
1996	1,5462	1,7114	0,1652	1,7168	1,4881	0,2287	1,6025
1997	1,7114	1,6480	-0,0634	1,7150	1,5648	0,1502	1,6399
1998	1,6480	1,6621	0,0141	1,7366	1,6057	0,1309	1,6712
1999	1,6621	1,6135	-0,0486	1,6797	1,5446	0,1351	1,6122
2000	1,6135	1,4935	-0,1200	1,6632	1,3931	0,2701	1,5282
2001	1,4935	1,4534	-0,0401	1,5106	1,3660	0,1446	1,4383
2002	1,4534	1,6076	0,1542	1,6136	1,4022	0,2114	1,5079
2003	1,6076	1,7853	0,1777	1,7933	1,5422	0,2511	1,6678
2004	1,7853	1,9196	0,1343	1,9548	1,7453	0,2095	1,8501
2005	1,9196	1,7184	-0,2012	1,9331	1,7014	0,2317	1,8173
2006	1,7184	1,9576	0,2392	1,9840	1,7165	0,2675	1,8503
2007	1,9576	1,9863	0,0287	2,1158	1,9133	0,2025	2,0146
2008	1,9863	1,4602	-0,5261	2,0406	1,4331	0,6075	1,7369
2009	1,4602	1,6126	0,1524	1,7024	1,3600	0,3424	1,5312
2010	1,6126	1,5584	-0,0542	1,6440	1,4206	0,2234	1,5323
2011	1,5584	1,5500	-0,0084	1,6732	1,5229	0,1503	1,5981
2012	1,5500	1,6231	0,0731	1,6314	1,5229	0,1085	1,5772
2013	1,6231	1,6552	0,0321	1,6577	1,4802	0,1775	1,5690
2014	1,6552	1,5570	-0,0982	1,7190	1,5470	0,1720	1,6330
2015	1,5570	1,4729	-0,0841	1,5936	1,4546	0,1390	1,5241
2016	1,4736	1,2338	-0,2398	1,5023	1,1452	0,3571	1,3238
2017	1,2346	1,3515	0,1169	1,3657	1,1981	0,1676	1,2819
2018	1,3514	1,2759	-0,0755	1,4379	1,2477	0,1902	1,3428
2019	1,2761						

Year	Open	Close	Difference (C-O)	Max	Min	Difference	Medium
1971	357,16	310,02	-47,14	357,16	314,40	42,76	335,78
1972	310,28	302,85	-7,43	310,28	263,13	47,15	286,71
1973	302,85	298,16	-4,69	302,85	262,65	40,20	282,75
1974	298,16	297,20	-0,96	301,68	275,77	25,91	288,73
1975	297,20	302,96	5,76	304,24	286,33	17,91	295,29
1976	302,96	287,61	-15,35	302,96	286,01	16,95	294,49
1977	287,61	241,09	-46,52	287,61	239,03	48,58	263,32
1978	241,09	201,71	-39,38	241,09	179,46	61,63	210,28
1979	201,71	238,69	36,98	248,96	201,71	47,25	225,34
1980	238,69	206,17	-32,52	250,67	202,74	47,93	226,71
1981	206,17	230,53	24,36	239,83	206,17	33,66	223,00
1982	230,53	239,57	9,04	276,79	230,53	46,26	253,66
1983	239,57	234,30	-5,27	246,10	231,11	14,99	238,61
1984	234,30	254,08	19,78	254,08	224,41	29,67	239,25
1985	254,08	191,53	-62,55	258,65	191,53	67,12	225,09
1986	191,53	156,90	-34,63	203,07	150,92	52,15	177,00
1987	156,90	127,73	-29,17	158,08	120,14	37,94	139,11
1988	127,73	124,31	-3,42	137,21	120,14	17,07	128,68
1989	124,31	144,04	19,73	151,63	122,04	29,59	136,84
1990	144,10	135,68	-8,42	159,96	123,06	36,90	141,51
1991	135,68	124,29	-11,39	142,30	124,29	18,01	133,30
1992	124,29	124,62	0,33	135,10	118,24	16,86	126,67
1993	124,62	111,34	-13,28	126,49	99,70	26,79	113,10
1994	111,34	99,49	-11,85	113,54	95,53	18,01	104,54
1995	99,49	103,20	3,71	107,45	79,56	27,89	93,51
1996	103,20	115,60	12,40	116,36	102,64	13,72	109,50
1997	115,60	130,25	14,65	131,37	110,08	21,29	120,73
1998	130,25	113,23	-17,02	147,65	111,19	36,46	129,42
1999	113,23	101,94	-11,29	124,71	100,83	23,88	112,77
2000	101,94	114,37	12,43	115,01	101,00	14,01	108,01
2001	114,37	131,46	17,09	135,26	113,36	21,90	124,31
2002	131,46	118,55	-12,91	135,13	115,13	20,00	125,13
2003	118,55	107,22	-11,33	121,83	106,57	15,26	114,20
2004	107,22	102,33	-4,89	114,90	101,68	13,22	108,29
2005	102,33	117,80	15,47	121,36	101,55	19,81	111,46
2006	117,80	118,96	1,16	119,92	108,77	11,15	114,35
2007	118,96	111,39	-7,57	124,25	106,99	17,26	115,62
2008	111,39	90,60	-20,79	111,99	87,00	24,99	99,50
2009	90,60	92,75	2,15	101,36	84,67	16,69	93,02
2010	92,75	80,97	-11,78	95,00	80,03	14,97	87,52
2011	80,97	76,73	-4,24	85,47	75,27	10,20	80,37
2012	76,73	86,52	9,79	86,88	75,66	11,22	81,27
2013	86,52	105,14	18,62	105,14	86,10	19,04	95,62
2014	105,14	119,53	14,39	122,00	100,34	21,66	111,17
2015	119,53	120,08	0,55	125,84	115,86	9,98	120,85
2016	120,30	116,89	-3,41	121,70	99,12	22,58	110,41
2017	116,92	112,69	-4,23	118,61	107,33	11,28	112,97
2018	112,67	109,58	-3,09	114,55	104,56	9,99	109,56
2019	109,57						

Appendix 4 Historical Data for XAU/USD (1971 – 2019)

Year	Open	Close	Difference (C-O)	Max	Min	Difference	Medium
1971	35,40	37,65	2,25	38,35	38,35	0,00	38,35
1972	44,30	65,20	20,90	68,60	47,45	21,15	58,03
1973	65,40	112,30	46,90	123,55	66,30	57,25	94,93
1974	116,80	186,75	69,95	186,75	132,80	53,95	159,78
1975	175,25	140,35	-34,90	182,00	140,35	41,65	161,18
1976	138,70	134,75	-3,95	134,75	104,35	30,40	119,55
1977	135,60	164,96	29,36	164,96	132,30	32,66	148,63
1978	169,20	226,00	56,80	242,60	176,10	66,50	209,35
1979	226,80	512,00	285,20	512,00	233,70	278,30	372,85
1980	512,00	586,00	74,00	637,00	495,00	142,00	566,00
1981	586,00	401,00	-185,00	513,75	401,00	112,75	457,38
1982	401,00	456,00	55,00	456,90	317,50	139,40	387,20
1983	452,00	381,50	-70,50	508,50	381,50	127,00	445,00
1984	383,00	308,30	-74,70	394,20	308,30	85,90	351,25
1985	305,50	329,70	24,20	333,20	287,70	45,50	310,45
1986	326,50	390,19	63,69	422,81	338,10	84,71	380,46
1987	406,90	485,85	78,95	492,67	403,43	89,24	448,05
1988	488,92	409,39	-79,53	488,92	394,03	94,89	441,48
1989	413,93	403,50	-10,43	411,70	358,29	53,41	385,00
1990	403,60	393,00	-10,60	418,20	356,80	61,40	387,50
1991	393,50	354,30	-39,20	370,20	348,30	21,90	359,25
1992	354,40	333,15	-21,25	357,85	333,00	24,85	345,43
1993	332,80	390,75	57,95	407,05	328,20	78,85	367,63
1994	390,55	382,85	-7,70	394,85	376,70	18,15	385,78
1995	382,90	387,10	4,20	391,00	374,85	16,15	382,93
1996	386,90	367,80	-19,10	406,45	367,80	38,65	387,13
1997	367,70	289,05	-78,65	367,70	288,80	78,90	328,25
1998	288,60	288,25	-0,35	306,65	276,40	30,25	291,53
1999	288,30	288,25	-0,05	299,50	255,30	44,20	277,40
2000	288,00	272,40	-15,60	292,12	264,80	27,32	278,46
2001	272,50	278,95	6,45	292,95	257,70	35,25	275,33
2002	278,60	347,00	68,40	347,00	282,10	64,90	314,55
2003	346,00	415,05	69,05	415,05	337,10	77,95	376,08
2004	415,00	438,45	23,45	450,88	387,20	63,68	419,04
2005	437,50	517,60	80,10	517,60	417,00	100,60	467,30
2006	516,75	636,80	120,05	730,40	516,75	213,65	623,58
2007	636,80	833,60	196,80	845,80	601,70	244,10	723,75
2008	833,30	880,20	46,90	1 031,20	682,80	348,40	857,00
2009	880,30	1 096,20	215,90	1 226,60	802,60	424,00	1 014,60
2010	1 096,75	1 421,45	324,70	1 432,95	1 044,15	388,80	1 238,55
2011	1 421,18	1 564,30	143,12	1 920,80	1 308,38	612,42	1 614,59
2012	1 566,12	1 674,95	108,83	1 796,19	1 529,00	267,19	1 662,60
2013	1 675,26	1 205,55	-469,71	1 696,37	1 181,82	514,55	1 439,10
2014	1 210,41	1 183,85	-26,56	1 392,37	1 132,16	260,21	1 262,27
2015	1 184,15	1 061,30	-122,85	1 306,85	1 046,23	260,62	1 176,54
2016	1 061,11	1 151,85	90,74	1 375,23	1 060,64	314,59	1 217,94
2017	1 150,53	1 302,55	152,02	1 357,89	1 145,80	212,09	1 251,85
2018	1 302,89	1 282,82	-20,07	1 366,47	1 160,34	206,13	1 263,41
2019	1 292,06						

Appendix 5 Historical Data for Crude Oil WTI Futures (M) CFD (1984 – 2019)

Year	Open	Close	Difference (C-O)	Max	Min	Difference	Medium
1984	29,25	26,41	-2,84	31,50	26,04	5,46	28,77
1985	26,15	26,30	0,15	31,82	24,66	7,16	28,24
1986	25,85	17,94	-7,91	26,60	9,75	16,85	18,18
1987	17,92	16,70	-1,22	22,76	14,90	7,86	18,83
1988	16,91	17,24	0,33	18,92	12,28	6,64	15,60
1989	17,17	21,82	4,65	25,30	16,95	8,35	21,13
1990	21,81	28,44	6,63	41,15	15,06	26,09	28,11
1991	28,07	19,12	-8,95	32,75	17,45	15,30	25,10
1992	19,10	19,50	0,40	22,95	17,72	5,23	20,34
1993	19,43	14,17	-5,26	21,14	13,75	7,39	17,45
1994	14,10	17,76	3,66	20,98	13,88	7,10	17,43
1995	17,65	19,55	1,90	20,82	16,60	4,22	18,71
1996	19,52	25,92	6,40	26,80	17,08	9,72	21,94
1997	25,88	17,64	-8,24	26,74	17,50	9,24	22,12
1998	17,68	12,05	-5,63	18,06	10,35	7,71	14,21
1999	12,15	25,60	13,45	27,15	11,26	15,89	19,21
2000	25,20	26,80	1,60	37,80	23,70	14,10	30,75
2001	26,90	19,84	-7,06	32,70	16,70	16,00	24,70
2002	19,20	31,20	12,00	33,65	17,85	15,80	25,75
2003	32,60	32,52	-0,08	39,99	25,04	14,95	32,52
2004	32,40	43,45	11,05	55,67	32,20	23,47	43,94
2005	43,10	61,04	17,94	70,85	41,25	29,60	56,05
2006	61,04	61,05	0,01	78,40	54,86	23,54	66,63
2007	60,98	95,98	35,00	99,29	49,90	49,39	74,60
2008	96,05	44,60	-51,45	147,27	32,40	114,87	89,84
2009	43,72	79,36	35,64	82,00	32,70	49,30	57,35
2010	79,63	91,38	11,75	92,06	64,24	27,82	78,15
2011	91,31	98,83	7,52	114,83	74,95	39,88	94,89
2012	99,70	91,82	-7,88	110,55	77,28	33,27	93,92
2013	91,78	98,42	6,64	112,24	85,61	26,63	98,93
2014	98,50	53,27	-45,23	107,73	52,44	55,29	80,09
2015	53,76	37,04	-16,72	62,58	33,98	28,60	48,28
2016	37,60	53,72	16,12	54,51	26,05	28,46	40,28
2017	54,20	60,42	6,22	60,51	42,05	18,46	51,28
2018	60,20	45,41	-14,79	76,90	42,36	34,54	59,63
2019	45,80						

Appendix 6 Historical Data for BTC/USD (2012 – 2019)

Year	Open	Close	Difference (C-O)	Max	Min	Difference	Medium
2012	6,10	13,50	7,40	13,70	4,20	9,50	8,95
2013	13,30	727,70	714,40	1 200,00	13,30	1 186,70	606,65
2014	740,00	317,00	-423,00	950,00	100,00	850,00	525,00
2015	317,50	429,00	111,50	503,40	171,00	332,40	337,20
2016	429,00	966,60	537,60	983,00	353,20	629,80	668,10
2017	966,60	13 800,00	12 833,40	19 891,00	738,70	19 152,30	10 314,85
2018	13 794,00	3 830,50	-9 963,50	17 252,00	3 219,20	14 032,80	10 235,60
2019	3 832,60						

Year	Open	Close	Difference (C-O)	Max	Min	Difference	Medium
1971	92,15	102,90	10,75	105,60	84,34	21,26	94,97
1972	102,09	118,05	15,96	119,79	100,87	18,92	110,33
1973	118,06	97,55	-20,51	121,74	91,05	30,69	106,40
1974	97,55	68,56	-28,99	101,05	60,96	40,09	81,01
1975	68,65	90,19	21,54	96,58	68,65	27,93	82,62
1976	100,11	107,46	7,35	108,72	89,81	18,91	99,27
1977	107,46	95,10	-12,36	107,97	90,01	17,96	98,99
1978	95,10	96,11	1,01	108,05	86,45	21,60	97,25
1979	96,11	107,94	11,83	112,16	95,22	16,94	103,69
1980	107,94	135,36	27,42	141,96	94,23	47,73	118,10
1981	135,76	122,55	-13,21	140,32	110,19	30,13	125,26
1982	122,55	140,64	18,09	144,36	102,20	42,16	123,28
1983	140,65	164,93	24,28	172,65	138,08	34,57	155,37
1984	164,93	167,24	2,31	170,41	147,26	23,15	158,84
1985	167,20	211,22	44,02	213,08	163,36	49,72	188,22
1986	211,28	242,17	30,89	254,24	202,60	51,64	228,42
1987	242,17	247,08	4,91	337,89	216,46	121,43	277,18
1988	247,10	277,72	30,62	283,85	240,17	43,68	262,01
1989	277,72	353,40	75,68	360,44	273,81	86,63	317,13
1990	353,40	330,22	-23,18	369,78	294,51	75,27	332,15
1991	330,20	417,09	86,89	418,32	309,55	108,77	363,94
1992	417,03	435,71	18,68	442,65	392,41	50,24	417,53
1993	435,70	466,45	30,75	471,29	426,88	44,41	449,09
1994	466,51	459,27	-7,24	482,85	435,86	46,99	459,36
1995	459,21	615,93	156,72	622,88	457,20	165,68	540,04
1996	615,93	740,74	124,81	762,12	597,29	164,83	679,71
1997	740,74	970,43	229,69	986,25	716,69	269,56	851,47
1998	970,43	1 229,23	258,80	1 244,93	912,83	332,10	1 078,88
1999	1 229,23	1 469,25	240,02	1 473,10	1 205,46	267,64	1 339,28
2000	1 469,25	1 320,28	-148,97	1 552,87	1 254,07	298,80	1 403,47
2001	1 320,28	1 148,08	-172,20	1 383,87	944,75	439,12	1 164,31
2002	1 148,08	879,82	-268,26	1 176,97	768,63	408,34	972,80
2003	879,92	1 111,92	232,00	1 112,56	788,90	323,66	950,73
2004	1 111,92	1 211,92	100,00	1 217,33	1 060,72	156,61	1 139,03
2005	1 211,92	1 248,29	36,37	1 275,80	1 136,15	139,65	1 205,98
2006	1 248,29	1 418,30	170,01	1 431,80	1 219,29	212,51	1 325,55
2007	1 418,03	1 468,36	50,33	1 576,09	1 363,08	213,01	1 469,59
2008	1 467,97	903,25	-564,72	1 471,77	741,02	730,75	1 106,40
2009	902,99	1 115,10	212,11	1 130,38	666,79	463,59	898,59
2010	1 116,56	1 257,64	141,08	1 262,60	1 010,91	251,69	1 136,76
2011	1 257,62	1 257,60	-0,02	1 370,58	1 074,77	295,81	1 222,68
2012	1 258,86	1 426,19	167,33	1 474,51	1 258,86	215,65	1 366,69
2013	1 426,19	1 848,36	422,17	1 849,44	1 426,19	423,25	1 637,82
2014	1 845,86	2 058,90	213,04	2 093,55	1 737,92	355,63	1 915,74
2015	2 058,90	2 043,94	-14,96	2 134,72	1 867,01	267,71	2 000,87
2016	2 038,20	2 238,83	200,63	2 277,53	1 810,10	467,43	2 043,82
2017	2 251,57	2 673,61	422,04	2 694,97	2 245,13	449,84	2 470,05
2018	2 683,73	2 506,85	-176,88	2 940,91	2 346,58	594,33	2 643,75
2019	2 476,96						

Appendix 8 Historical Data FTSE100 (2002 - 2019)

Year	Open	Close	Difference (C-O)	Max	Min	Difference	Medium
2002	5 217,40	3 940,40	-1 277,00	5 362,30	3 609,90	1 752,40	4 486,10
2003	3 940,40	4 476,90	536,50	4 491,80	3 277,50	1 214,30	3 884,65
2004	4 476,90	4 814,30	337,40	4 826,20	4 283,00	543,20	4 554,60
2005	4 814,30	5 618,76	804,46	5 647,20	4 773,70	873,50	5 210,45
2006	5 618,80	6 220,81	602,01	6 271,40	5 467,40	804,00	5 869,40
2007	6 220,80	6 456,91	236,11	6 754,10	5 821,70	932,40	6 287,90
2008	6 456,90	4 434,17	-2 022,73	6 534,70	3 665,21	2 869,49	5 099,96
2009	4 434,17	5 412,88	978,71	5 445,17	3 460,71	1 984,46	4 452,94
2010	5 412,88	5 899,94	487,06	6 021,46	4 790,04	1 231,42	5 405,75
2011	5 899,94	5 572,28	-327,66	6 105,77	4 791,01	1 314,76	5 448,39
2012	5 572,28	5 897,81	325,53	5 997,04	5 229,76	767,28	5 613,40
2013	5 897,81	6 749,09	851,28	6 875,62	5 897,81	977,81	6 386,72
2014	6 749,09	6 566,09	-183,00	6 904,86	6 072,68	832,18	6 488,77
2015	6 566,09	6 242,32	-323,77	7 122,74	5 768,22	1 354,52	6 445,48
2016	6 242,32	7 142,83	900,51	7 142,83	5 499,51	1 643,32	6 321,17
2017	7 142,83	7 687,77	544,94	7 697,62	7 093,57	604,05	7 395,60
2018	7 687,77	7 001,94	-685,83	7 908,50	6 536,53	1 371,97	7 222,52
2019	7 001,94						

Year	Open	Close	Difference (C-O)	Max	Min	Difference	Medium
1971	1,1219	1,1874	0,0655	1,1874	1,1219	0,0655	1,1547
1972	1,1874	1,2719	0,0845	1,2719	1,1874	0,0845	1,2297
1973	1,2719	1,4814	0,2095	1,4814	1,2699	0,2115	1,3757
1974	1,4814	1,3235	-0,1579	1,4864	1,3066	0,1798	1,3965
1975	1,3235	1,2556	-0,0679	1,3643	1,2530	0,1113	1,3087
1976	1,2556	1,1063	-0,1493	1,2594	1,0113	0,2481	1,1354
1977	1,1063	1,1397	0,0334	1,1397	1,1063	0,0334	1,1230
1978	1,1397	1,1330	-0,0067	1,1857	1,1291	0,0566	1,1574
1979	1,1330	1,1050	-0,0280	1,1330	1,0934	0,0396	1,1132
1980	1,1050	1,1806	0,0756	1,1806	1,0805	0,1001	1,1306
1981	1,1806	1,1264	-0,0542	1,1806	1,1264	0,0542	1,1535
1982	1,1264	0,9763	-0,1501	1,1264	0,9339	0,1925	1,0302
1983	0,9763	0,8944	-0,0819	0,9763	0,8608	0,1155	0,9186
1984	0,8944	0,8227	-0,0717	0,9412	0,8227	0,1185	0,8820
1985	0,8227	0,6792	-0,1435	0,9227	0,6428	0,2799	0,7828
1986	0,6792	0,6637	-0,0155	0,7396	0,5948	0,1448	0,6672
1987	0,6637	0,7208	0,0571	0,7350	0,6375	0,0975	0,6863
1988	0,7208	0,8525	0,1317	0,8836	0,6923	0,1913	0,7880
1989	0,8525	0,7871	-0,0654	0,8959	0,7324	0,1635	0,8142
1990	0,7871	0,7714	-0,0157	0,8495	0,7383	0,1112	0,7939
1991	0,7714	0,7578	-0,0136	0,8077	0,7480	0,0597	0,7779
1992	0,7578	0,6876	-0,0702	0,7709	0,6765	0,0944	0,7237
1993	0,6876	0,6780	-0,0096	0,7269	0,6400	0,0869	0,6835
1994	0,6780	0,7751	0,0971	0,7797	0,6758	0,1039	0,7278
1995	0,7751	0,7428	-0,0323	0,7767	0,7060	0,0707	0,7414
1996	0,7428	0,7939	0,0511	0,8214	0,7301	0,0913	0,7758
1997	0,7939	0,6514	-0,1425	0,7999	0,6447	0,1552	0,7223
1998	0,6514	0,6113	-0,0401	0,6892	0,5482	0,1410	0,6187
1999	0,6113	0,6554	0,0441	0,6751	0,6094	0,0657	0,6423
2000	0,6554	0,5578	-0,0976	0,6694	0,5053	0,1641	0,5874
2001	0,5578	0,5078	-0,0500	0,5724	0,4759	0,0965	0,5242
2002	0,5078	0,5602	0,0524	0,5806	0,5031	0,0775	0,5419
2003	0,5602	0,7513	0,1911	0,7548	0,5574	0,1974	0,6561
2004	0,7513	0,7813	0,0300	0,8007	0,6764	0,1243	0,7386
2005	0,7813	0,7324	-0,0489	0,7981	0,7207	0,0774	0,7594
2006	0,7324	0,7875	0,0551	0,7926	0,6983	0,0943	0,7455
2007	0,7875	0,8637	0,0762	0,9398	0,7656	0,1742	0,8527
2008	0,8637	0,7040	-0,1597	0,9847	0,5992	0,3855	0,7920
2009	0,7040	0,8954	0,1914	0,9394	0,6217	0,3177	0,7806
2010	0,8954	1,0193	0,1239	1,0248	0,8049	0,2199	0,9149
2011	1,0193	1,0207	0,0014	1,1078	0,9363	0,1715	1,0221
2012	1,0207	1,0392	0,0185	1,0846	0,9564	0,1282	1,0205
2013	1,0392	0,8902	-0,1490	1,0595	0,8806	0,1789	0,9701
2014	0,8902	0,8156	-0,0746	0,9501	0,8052	0,1449	0,8777
2015	0,8156	0,7263	-0,0893	0,8295	0,6881	0,1414	0,7588
2016	0,7284	0,7216	-0,0068	0,7836	0,6826	0,1010	0,7331
2017	0,7227	0,7802	0,0575	0,8125	0,7162	0,0963	0,7644
2018	0,7802	0,7052	-0,0750	0,8136	0,7016	0,1120	0,7576
2019	0,7048						

Appendix 10 Historical Data for USD/RUB (1994 - 2019)

Year	Open	Close	Difference (C-O)	Max	Min	Difference	Medium
1994	2,6642	3,9946	1,3304	3,9946	2,6642	1,3304	3,3294
1995	3,9946	4,6717	0,6771	5,1098	3,9946	1,1152	4,5522
1996	4,6717	5,5830	0,9113	5,5830	4,6717	0,9113	5,1274
1997	5,5830	5,9934	0,4104	5,9934	5,5830	0,4104	5,7882
1998	5,9493	21,3700	15,4207	25,6853	5,9493	19,7360	15,8173
1999	21,3700	27,4323	6,0623	27,6864	20,7673	6,9191	24,2269
2000	27,4323	28,4229	0,9906	29,1270	26,7584	2,3686	27,9427
2001	28,4229	30,4537	2,0308	30,5328	27,8428	2,6900	29,1878
2002	30,4537	31,9195	1,4658	31,9837	30,1487	1,8350	31,0662
2003	31,9195	29,2122	-2,7073	31,9698	29,1098	2,8600	30,5398
2004	29,2122	27,7144	-1,4978	29,2935	27,6651	1,6284	28,4793
2005	27,8275	28,7128	0,8853	29,0038	27,4013	1,6025	28,2026
2006	28,7128	26,3132	-2,3996	28,7643	26,0844	2,6799	27,4244
2007	26,3132	24,5634	-1,7498	26,6334	24,1852	2,4482	25,4093
2008	24,5634	30,4447	5,8813	30,7023	22,9746	7,7277	26,8385
2009	30,4447	30,2975	-0,1472	36,5901	28,4576	8,1325	32,5239
2010	30,2975	30,5551	0,2576	31,9903	28,7888	3,2015	30,3896
2011	30,5551	32,1535	1,5984	32,9096	27,0502	5,8594	29,9799
2012	32,1535	30,5492	-1,6043	34,1077	28,7795	5,3282	31,4436
2013	30,5492	32,7795	2,2303	33,6009	29,7222	3,8787	31,6616
2014	32,7795	58,0501	25,2706	80,0306	32,4527	47,5779	56,2417
2015	58,0501	72,7845	14,7344	74,4183	48,4264	25,9919	61,4224
2016	73,5963	61,2730	-12,3233	85,7520	60,1189	25,6331	72,9355
2017	61,2730	57,6130	-3,6600	61,2865	55,7253	5,5612	58,5059
2018	57,6114	69,8319	12,2205	70,5896	55,5655	15,0241	63,0776
2019	69,8319						

Year	Open	Close	Difference (C-O)	Max	Min	Difference	Medium
1971	4,2906	3,8652	-0,4254	4,3001	3,9067	0,3934	4,1034
1972	3,8652	3,6109	-0,2543	3,8704	3,6109	0,2595	3,7407
1973	3,6109	3,2477	-0,3632	3,6109	2,8326	0,7783	3,2218
1974	3,2477	2,4850	-0,7627	3,2477	2,4850	0,7627	2,8664
1975	2,4850	2,5929	0,1079	2,7370	2,3974	0,3396	2,5672
1976	2,5929	2,4984	-0,0945	2,5929	2,4286	0,1643	2,5108
1977	2,4996	1,9696	-0,5300	2,5506	1,9696	0,5810	2,2601
1978	1,9696	1,6964	-0,2732	1,9696	1,4876	0,4820	1,7286
1979	1,6964	1,6280	-0,0684	1,7204	1,5492	0,1712	1,6348
1980	1,6280	1,9190	0,2910	1,9190	1,6247	0,2943	1,7719
1981	1,9190	1,8565	-0,0625	2,1387	1,7643	0,3744	1,9515
1982	1,8565	2,0134	0,1569	2,2039	1,8565	0,3474	2,0302
1983	2,0134	2,2484	0,2350	2,2484	2,0134	0,2350	2,1309
1984	2,2484	2,6743	0,4259	2,6743	2,1475	0,5268	2,4109
1985	2,6743	2,0216	-0,6527	2,6743	2,0216	0,6527	2,3480
1986	2,0216	1,5393	-0,4823	2,0216	1,5393	0,4823	1,7805
1987	1,5393	1,3655	-0,1738	1,6306	1,2611	0,3695	1,4459
1988	1,3655	1,5958	0,2303	1,6149	1,2611	0,3538	1,4380
1989	1,5958	1,4996	-0,0962	1,8083	1,4823	0,3260	1,6453
1990	1,5012	1,2713	-0,2299	1,5909	1,2335	0,3574	1,4122
1991	1,2713	1,3578	0,0865	1,5928	1,2273	0,3655	1,4101
1992	1,3578	1,4623	0,1045	1,5504	1,2044	0,3460	1,3774
1993	1,4623	1,4870	0,0247	1,5540	1,3770	0,1770	1,4655
1994	1,4870	1,3077	-0,1793	1,4962	1,2335	0,2627	1,3649
1995	1,3077	1,1521	-0,1556	1,3187	1,1063	0,2124	1,2125
1996	1,1521	1,3416	0,1895	1,4368	1,1445	0,2923	1,2907
1997	1,3416	1,4589	0,1173	1,5394	1,3344	0,2050	1,4369
1998	1,4589	1,3759	-0,0830	1,5492	1,2709	0,2783	1,4101
1999	1,3583	1,5892	0,2309	1,6013	1,3340	0,2673	1,4677
2000	1,5992	1,6104	0,0112	1,7942	1,5375	0,2567	1,6659
2001	1,6104	1,6590	0,0486	1,8216	1,5613	0,2603	1,6915
2002	1,6590	1,3801	-0,2789	1,7247	1,3750	0,3497	1,5499
2003	1,3801	1,2372	-0,1429	1,4271	1,2271	0,2000	1,3271
2004	1,2372	1,1373	-0,0999	1,3228	1,1240	0,1988	1,2234
2005	1,1373	1,3112	0,1739	1,3291	1,1311	0,1980	1,2301
2006	1,3123	1,2175	-0,0948	1,3233	1,1852	0,1381	1,2543
2007	1,2175	1,1316	-0,0859	1,2575	1,0873	0,1702	1,1724
2008	1,1316	1,0676	-0,0640	1,2290	0,9643	0,2647	1,0967
2009	1,0676	1,0334	-0,0342	1,1964	0,9885	0,2079	1,0925
2010	1,0334	0,9311	-0,1023	1,1724	0,9254	0,2470	1,0489
2011	0,9311	0,9356	0,0045	0,9782	0,7055	0,2727	0,8419
2012	0,9356	0,9134	-0,0222	0,9952	0,8881	0,1071	0,9417
2013	0,9134	0,8919	-0,0215	0,9830	0,8767	0,1063	0,9299
2014	0,8919	0,9932	0,1013	0,9949	0,8667	0,1282	0,9308
2015	0,9932	1,0006	0,0074	1,0330	0,7327	0,3003	0,8829
2016	1,0014	1,0184	0,0170	1,0350	0,9442	0,0908	0,9896
2017	1,0197	0,9744	-0,0453	1,0336	0,9421	0,0915	0,9879
2018	0,9745	0,9816	0,0071	1,0130	0,9188	0,0942	0,9659
2019	0,9816						

Appendix 12 Historical Data for USD/CAD (1982 - 2019)

Year	Open	Close	Difference (C-O)	Max	Min	Difference	Medium
1982	1,1969	1,2362	0,0393	1,2923	1,1969	0,0954	1,2446
1983	1,2362	1,2488	0,0126	1,2488	1,2259	0,0229	1,2374
1984	1,2488	1,3261	0,0773	1,3261	1,2488	0,0773	1,2875
1985	1,3261	1,4223	0,0962	1,4223	1,3261	0,0962	1,3742
1986	1,4223	1,3802	-0,0421	1,4223	1,3621	0,0602	1,3922
1987	1,3802	1,2972	-0,0830	1,3802	1,2935	0,0867	1,3369
1988	1,2972	1,1903	-0,1069	1,2981	1,1814	0,1167	1,2398
1989	1,1903	1,1565	-0,0338	1,2185	1,1541	0,0644	1,1863
1990	1,1565	1,1594	0,0029	1,2092	1,1260	0,0832	1,1676
1991	1,1594	1,1552	-0,0042	1,1667	1,1180	0,0487	1,1424
1992	1,1552	1,2700	0,1148	1,2967	1,1393	0,1574	1,2180
1993	1,2700	1,3215	0,0515	1,3484	1,2390	0,1094	1,2937
1994	1,3257	1,4015	0,0758	1,4090	1,3063	0,1027	1,3577
1995	1,4006	1,3636	-0,0370	1,4276	1,3261	0,1015	1,3769
1996	1,3615	1,3696	0,0081	1,3873	1,3245	0,0628	1,3559
1997	1,3679	1,4284	0,0605	1,4417	1,3320	0,1097	1,3869
1998	1,4284	1,5310	0,1026	1,5847	1,4030	0,1817	1,4939
1999	1,5310	1,4489	-0,0821	1,5472	1,4405	0,1067	1,4939
2000	1,4489	1,4979	0,0490	1,5627	1,4299	0,1328	1,4963
2001	1,4979	1,5927	0,0948	1,6053	1,4863	0,1190	1,5458
2002	1,5927	1,5705	-0,0222	1,6194	1,5009	0,1185	1,5602
2003	1,5705	1,2945	-0,2760	1,5791	1,2822	0,2969	1,4307
2004	1,2945	1,2001	-0,0944	1,3997	1,1685	0,2312	1,2841
2005	1,2001	1,1628	-0,0373	1,2719	1,1391	0,1328	1,2055
2006	1,1628	1,1653	0,0025	1,1840	1,0904	0,0936	1,1372
2007	1,1653	0,9971	-0,1682	1,1870	0,9041	0,2829	1,0456
2008	0,9971	1,2153	0,2182	1,3015	0,9688	0,3327	1,1352
2009	1,2153	1,0518	-0,1635	1,3061	1,0179	0,2882	1,1620
2010	1,0518	0,9939	-0,0579	1,0845	0,9895	0,0950	1,0370
2011	0,9939	1,0190	0,0251	1,0648	0,9392	0,1256	1,0020
2012	1,0190	0,9910	-0,0280	1,0439	0,9611	0,0828	1,0025
2013	0,9910	1,0608	0,0698	1,0727	0,9790	0,0937	1,0259
2014	1,0608	1,1606	0,0998	1,2830	1,0554	0,2276	1,1692
2015	1,1606	1,3824	0,2218	1,3997	1,1563	0,2434	1,2780
2016	1,3841	1,3433	-0,0408	1,4691	1,2459	0,2232	1,3575
2017	1,3438	1,2579	-0,0859	1,3795	1,2060	0,1735	1,2928
2018	1,2579	1,3638	0,1059	1,3664	1,2248	0,1416	1,2956
2019	1,3636						

Appendix 13 Historical Data for USD/KZT (1995 - 2019)

Year	Open	Close	Difference (C-O)	Max	Min	Difference	Medium
1995	62,5000	63,7600	1,2600	64,2650	54,0000	10,2650	59,1325
1996	63,9900	74,0000	10,0100	74,0100	63,9000	10,1100	68,9550
1997	74,4800	76,4900	2,0100	76,7700	73,8800	2,8900	75,3250
1998	76,0000	84,5000	8,5000	84,6000	75,3700	9,2300	79,9850
1999	84,1500	138,4000	54,2500	142,5500	83,4500	59,1000	113,0000
2000	137,8900	145,5550	7,6650	145,6550	137,8800	7,7750	141,7675
2001	145,3500	150,9000	5,5500	151,0600	144,0100	7,0500	147,5350
2002	151,0500	155,8500	4,8000	156,6100	150,5000	6,1100	153,5550
2003	155,8700	143,2700	-12,6000	156,0150	143,1200	12,8950	149,5675
2004	143,2100	129,9600	-13,2500	143,5650	129,6000	13,9650	136,5825
2005	129,9600	133,6750	3,7150	136,4450	129,0000	7,4450	132,7225
2006	133,6800	126,9250	-6,7550	133,8500	116,7700	17,0800	125,3100
2007	126,8000	120,7200	-6,0800	126,9350	118,7000	8,2350	122,8175
2008	120,6900	121,1250	0,4350	121,1750	119,4150	1,7600	120,2950
2009	120,8750	148,5200	27,6450	151,0500	120,0250	31,0250	135,5375
2010	148,4900	147,3700	-1,1200	148,8500	146,0700	2,7800	147,4600
2011	147,5050	148,4850	0,9800	148,4850	145,1200	3,3650	146,8025
2012	148,4750	150,0700	1,5950	151,8600	146,8450	5,0150	149,3525
2013	150,0700	154,3500	4,2800	154,6300	149,0000	5,6300	151,8150
2014	154,2000	182,8650	28,6650	186,2250	154,2000	32,0250	170,2125
2015	182,7900	340,6000	157,8100	350,1000	182,3400	167,7600	266,2200
2016	340,9100	333,6850	-7,2250	392,0500	326,4200	65,6300	359,2350
2017	333,3550	332,8050	-0,5500	345,7550	309,5250	36,2300	327,6400
2018	332,5400	384,3300	51,7900	384,8300	318,0350	66,7950	351,4325
2019	383,1800						

Appendix 14 Historical Chart: Silver Futures (CFD) (1974 - 2019)

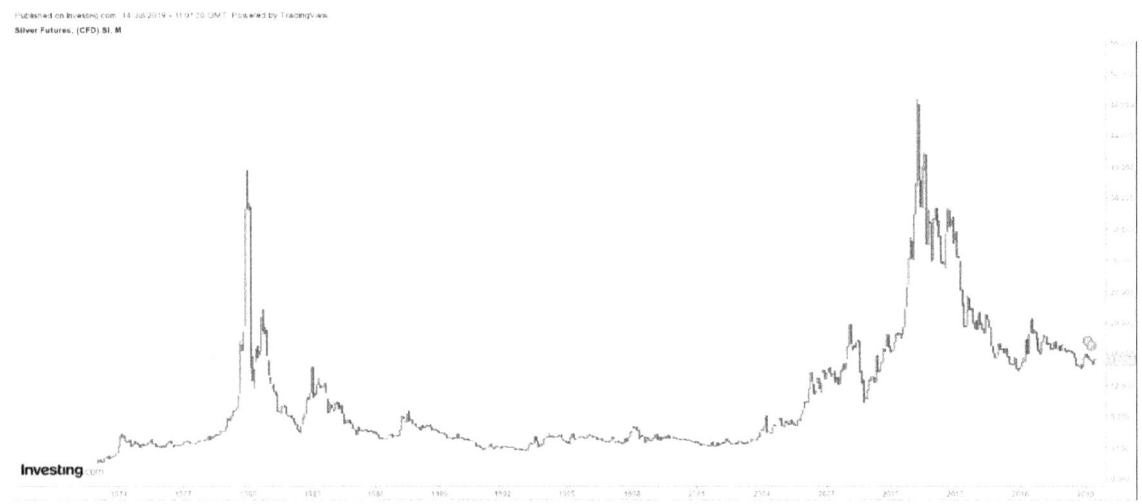

Appendix 15 Historical Chart: Crude Oil WTI Futures vs. USD/KZT (CFD) (1995 - 2018)

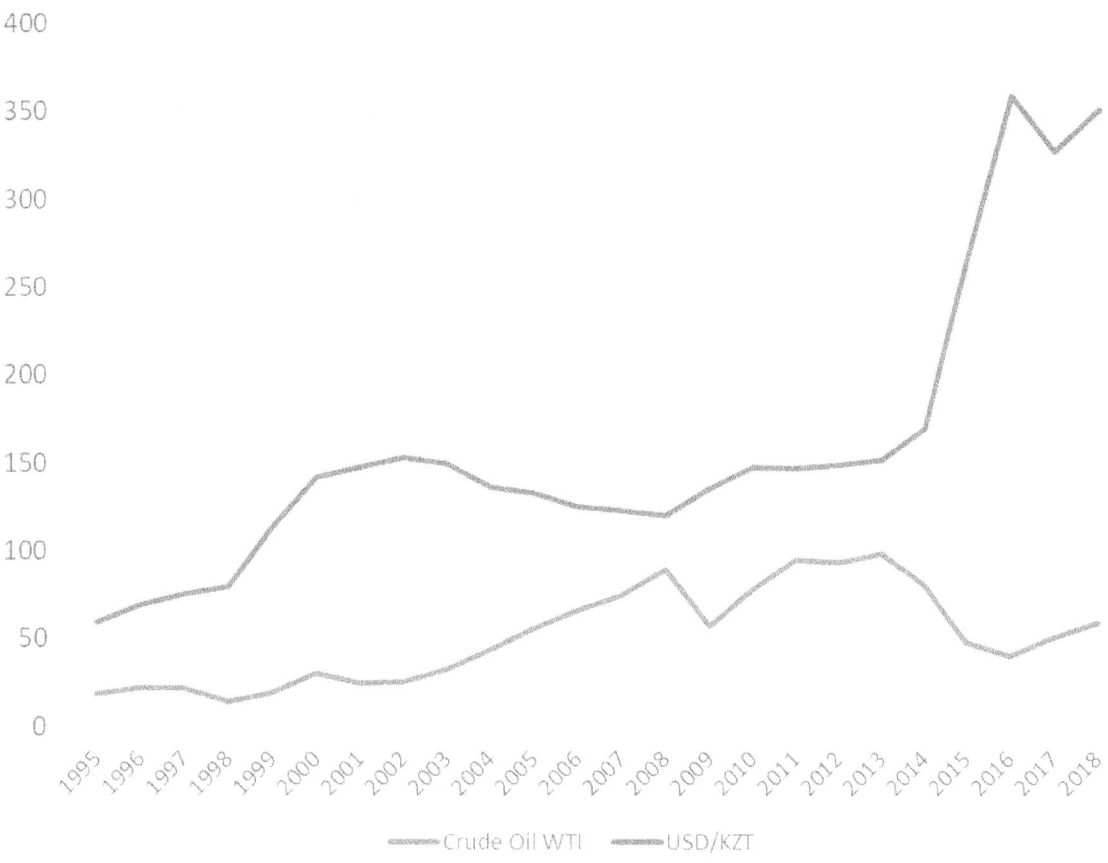

Appendix 16 EUR/GBP historical dynamics

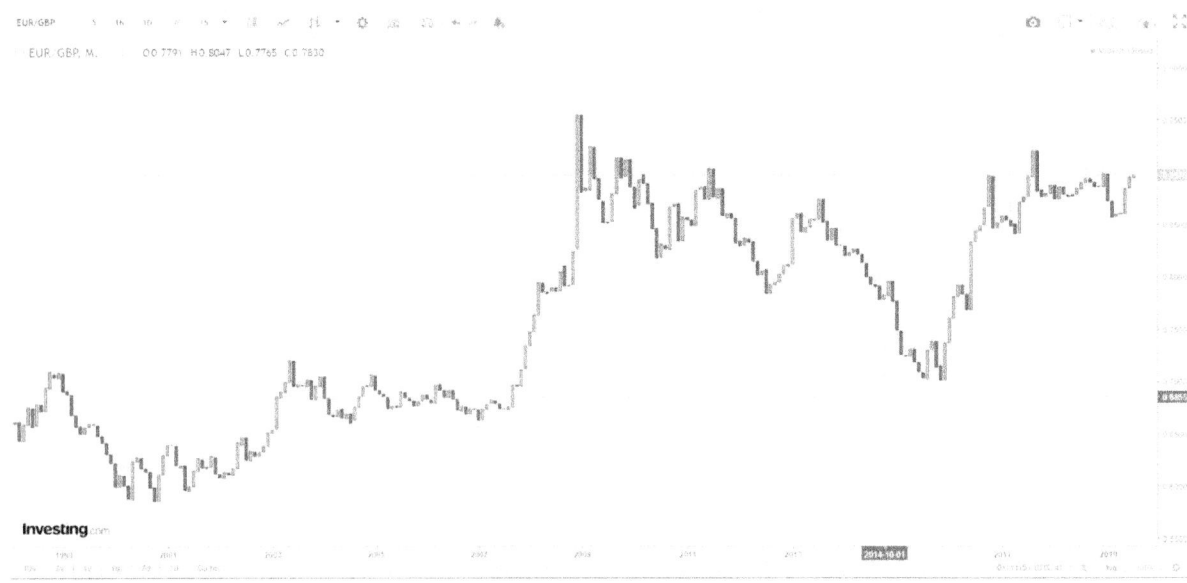

Auckland	Токио	Astana/Almaty	London	New-York
9:00	6:00	3:00	21:00	**16:00**
10:00	7:00	4:00	22:00	**17:00**
11:00	8:00	5:00	23:00	18:00
12:00	**9:00**	6:00	0:00	19:00
13:00	**10:00**	7:00	1:00	20:00
14:00	**11:00**	8:00	2:00	21:00
15:00	**12:00**	**9:00**	3:00	22:00
16:00	**13:00**	**10:00**	4:00	23:00
17:00	**14:00**	**11:00**	5:00	0:00
18:00	**15:00**	**12:00**	6:00	1:00
19:00	**16:00**	**13:00**	7:00	2:00
20:00	**17:00**	**14:00**	8:00	3:00
21:00	18:00	**15:00**	**9:00**	4:00
22:00	19:00	**16:00**	**10:00**	5:00
23:00	20:00	**17:00**	**11:00**	6:00
0:00	21:00	18:00	**12:00**	7:00
1:00	22:00	19:00	**13:00**	8:00
2:00	23:00	20:00	**14:00**	**9:00**
3:00	0:00		**15:00**	**10:00**
4:00	1:00		**16:00**	**11:00**
5:00	2:00		**17:00**	**12:00**
6:00	3:00	0:00	18:00	**13:00**
7:00	4:00	1:00	19:00	**14:00**
8:00	5:00	2:00	20:00	**15:00**
9:00	6:00	3:00	21:00	**16:00**
10:00	7:00	4:00	22:00	**17:00**
11:00	8:00	5:00	23:00	18:00

Appendix 18 Exchange Names, Abbreviations, Time Zones and Working Hours

Exchange Name	Time Zone	Opening Time	Closing Time	Closed for Lunch
Australian Securities Exchange (ASX)	(UTC+10, DST)	10:00	16:10	No
Euronext Amsterdam (AMS)	(UTC+1, DST)	9:00	17:40	No
Euronext Paris (EPA)	(UTC+1, DST)	9:00	17:30	No
Frankfurt Stock Exchange, Xetra (trading system), Eurex	(UTC+1, DST)	8:00 (Eurex) 9:00 (floor) 9:00 (Xetra)	22:00 (Eurex) 20:00 (floor) 17:30 (Xetra)	No
Hong Kong Stock Exchange (HKEX)	(UTC+8)	10:00	16:00	12:30-14:30
Bombay Stock Exchange (BSE)	(UTC+5.5)	9:55	15:30	No
Johannesburg (JSE)	(UTC+2)	9:00	17:00	No
London Stock Exchange (LSE)	(UTC+0, DST)	8:00	16:30	No
NASDAQ	(UTC-5, DST)	9:30	16:00	No
NYSE	(UTC-5, DST)	9:30	16:00	No
NZSX	(UTC+12, DST)	10:00	17:00	No
Oslo Stock Exchange (OSE)	(UTC+1, DST)	9:00	17:30	No
Singapore Exchange (SGX)	(UTC+8)	9:00	17:00	12:30-14:00
Stockholm Stock Exchange (OMX)	(CET+1, UTC+2)	9:00	17:30	No
Swiss Exchange (SIX)	(UTC+1, DST)	9:00	17:30	No
Amman Stock Exchange (ASE)	(CET+1, UTC+2)	10:00	12:00	No
Toronto Stock Exchange (TSX)	(UTC-5, DST)	9:30	16:00	No
Tokyo Stock Exchange (TSE)	(UTC+9)	9:00	15:00	11:00-12:30
Copenhagen Stock Exchange (CSE)	(UTC+1, DST)	9:00	17:00	No

Source: Forex.com

Appendix 19 Top 30 Cryptocurrencies

#	Name	Symbol	Price (USD)	Market Cap	Vol (24H)	Total Vol	Chg (24H)	Chg (7D)
1	Bitcoin	BTC	10,645.5	$190.76B	$19.26B	31.17%	+0.89%	-3.18%
2	Ethereum	ETH	222.35	$24.34B	$6.98B	11.29%	+0.60%	-11.64%
3	XRP	XRP	0.32733	$14.18B	$1.13B	1.84%	+1.55%	+1.74%
4	Litecoin	LTC	98.218	$6.25B	$3.60B	5.82%	+1.01%	+1.98%
5	Bitcoin Cash	BCH	320.26	$5.84B	$1.69B	2.73%	+5.10%	-2.42%
6	Binance Coin	BNB	30.035	$4.80B	$354.06M	0.57%	+0.30%	+0.62%
7	Tether	USDT	0.9984	$4.04B	$20.68B	33.47%	-0.15%	+0.13%
8	EOS	EOS	4.2212	$3.96B	$1.82B	2.94%	+2.33%	-7.02%
9	Bitcoin SV	BSV	171.68	$3.22B	$672.07M	1.09%	+12.15%	+23.45%
10	TRON	TRX	0.028365	$1.98B	$602.33M	0.97%	+5.30%	+5.01%
11	Stellar	XLM	0.09136	$1.82B	$185.88M	0.30%	+0.35%	-0.11%
12	Cardano	ADA	0.060878	$1.63B	$67.01M	0.11%	+2.96%	-2.96%
13	Monero	XMR	85.213	$1.46B	$112.31M	0.18%	+2.66%	-6.42%
14	UNUS SED LEO	LEO	1.3076	$1.33B	$9.58M	0.02%	+7.70%	-6.10%
15	Dash	DASH	116.89	$1.06B	$164.51M	0.27%	+1.51%	-12.69%
16	NEO	NEO	13.022	$929.77M	$423.90M	0.69%	+1.44%	-2.94%
17	Chainlink	LINK	2.5	$915.96M	$57.17M	0.09%	-2.22%	-15.59%
18	IOTA	MIOTA	0.31549	$895.92M	$14.23M	0.02%	-0.13%	-2.93%
19	Cosmos	ATOM	4.1868	$808.36M	$179.73M	0.29%	+6.04%	+2.53%
20	Tezos	XTZ	1.13755	$716.00M	$6.08M	0.01%	+8.57%	+10.46%
21	Ethereum Classic	ETC	6.2212	$688.47M	$512.78M	0.83%	+1.21%	-2.85%
22	NEM	XEM	0.06807	$616.24M	$32.28M	0.05%	-0.02%	-1.70%
23	Maker	MKR	569.31	$568.23M	$1.86M	0%	-0.57%	-10.64%
24	Ontology	ONT	1.0161	$555.93M	$160.41M	0.26%	+7.77%	+1.54%
25	Zcash	ZEC	75.49	$535.75M	$219.68M	0.36%	-0.31%	-12.22%
26	Bitcoin Gold	BTG	26.61	$468.82M	$19.84M	0.03%	+0.55%	-5.23%
27	Crypto.com Chain	CRO	0.0566	$446.01M	$3.54M	0.01%	-4.06%	-25.20%
28	USD Coin	USDC	1.00159	$404.75M	$100.45M	0.16%	-0.46%	+0.06%
29	INO COIN	INO	2.23162	$401.70M	$1.65M	0%	+1.50%	+31.17%
30	V Systems	VSYS	0.21844	$394.71M	$13.45M	0.02%	-4.30%	+0.02%
31	Dogecoin	DOGE	0.003094	$373.33M	$22.04M	0.04%	+0.51%	-2.85%
32	Egretia	EGT	0.08399	$343.32M	$50.08M	0.08%	+8.99%	-7.24%
33	VeChain	VET	0.005956	$335.03M	$26.19M	0.04%	+0.43%	-3.21%
34	Basic Attention Token	BAT	0.24708	$320.18M	$21.41M	0.03%	-0.64%	-9.01%
35	Silverway	SLV	1.037	$312.94M	$2.51M	0%	+1.25%	-45.36%
36	Qtum	QTUM	3.1879	$311.79M	$255.11M	0.41%	+3.16%	-5.27%
37	Decred	DCR	28.978	$296.33M	$2.37M	0%	-0.52%	-3.08%
38	OmiseGO	OMG	1.6976	$244.56M	$80.62M	0.13%	+7.66%	-1.15%
39	Huobi Token	HT	4.3734	$217.95M	$84.58M	0.14%	+0.62%	+8.23%
40	BitTorrent	BTT	0.001005	$215.50M	$40.57M	0.07%	+1.05%	-9.46%
41	TrueUSD	TUSD	0.9999	$208.64M	$112.52M	0.18%	+0.07%	+0.03%
42	HedgeTrade	HEDG	0.6752	$200.81M	$1.76M	0%	+2.45%	+1.83%
43	Ravencoin	RVN	0.0472	$190.75M	$15.31M	0.02%	+2.03%	+2.53%
44	Lisk	LSK	1.5164	$178.25M	$9.72M	0.02%	+11.93%	+7.64%
45	Paxos Standard Token	PAX	1.0005	$177.18M	$107.36M	0.17%	+0.04%	-0.04%
46	Holo	HOT	0.001288	$176.38M	$6.22M	0.01%	+2.10%	-5.82%
47	Bitcoin Diamond	BCD	0.84772	$161.82M	$4.85M	0.01%	+2.73%	-8.06%
48	Nano	NANO	1.1954	$159.19M	$11.33M	0.02%	+6.62%	+6.84%
49	ICON	ICX	0.26574	$158.52M	$8.57M	0.01%	-1.44%	-26.00%
50	Aurora	AOA	0.023097	$152.99M	$7.92M	0.01%	-1.78%	+1.18%

Source: www.investing.com

Appendix 20 Historical Stock Prices of Amazon.com

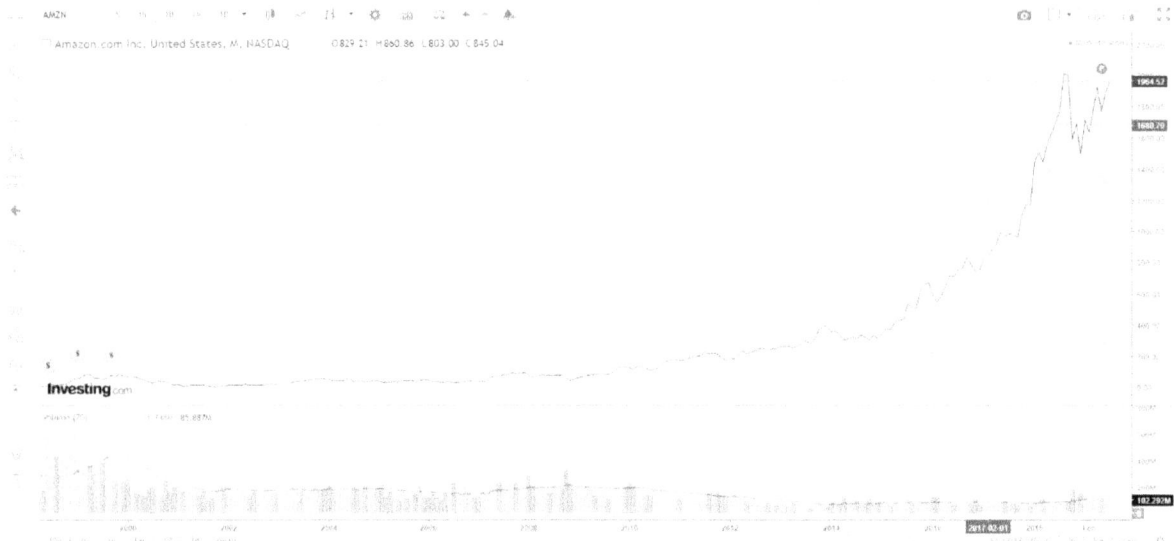

Appendix 21 Historical Stock Prices of Apple Inc.

Appendix 22 List of S&P500 companies (07/18/2019)

#	Company	Symbol	Weight		Price	Change
1	Microsoft Corporation	MSFT	4.202792	▼	136.55	-0.07(-0.05%)
2	Apple Inc.	AAPL	3.614141	▼	202.40	-0.19(-0.09%)
3	Amazon.com Inc.	AMZN	3.288515	▼	1,960.50	-4.02(-0.20%)
4	Facebook Inc. Class A	FB	1.939390	▲	198.44	0.08(0.04%)
5	Berkshire Hathaway Inc. Class B	BRK.B	1.619593	▼	205.52	-0.45(-0.22%)
6	JPMorgan Chase & Co.	JPM	1.495529	▼	113.35	-0.19(-0.17%)
7	Alphabet Inc. Class C	GOOG	1.412465	▼	1,129.50	-0.60(-0.05%)
8	Johnson & Johnson	JNJ	1.409773	▼	130.20	-0.11(-0.08%)
9	Alphabet Inc. Class A	GOOGL	1.381194	▼	1,129.17	-2.38(-0.21%)
10	Exxon Mobil Corporation	XOM	1.273089	▼	74.86	-0.13(-0.17%)
11	Visa Inc. Class A	V	1.262159	▼	178.71	-0.53(-0.30%)
12	Procter & Gamble Company	PG	1.164159	▲	115.10	0.09(0.08%)
13	Bank of America Corp	BAC	1.048046	▼	29.35	-0.05(-0.17%)
14	Mastercard Incorporated Class A	MA	1.001220	▼	275.05	-0.55(-0.20%)
15	UnitedHealth Group Incorporated	UNH	0.995673	▼	256.47	-0.18(-0.07%)
16	Walt Disney Company	DIS	0.994017	▲	139.95	0.10(0.07%)
17	Cisco Systems Inc.	CSCO	0.993721	▼	57.12	-0.24(-0.42%)
18	AT&T Inc.	T	0.970895	▼	32.75	-0.04(-0.12%)
19	Pfizer Inc.	PFE	0.961124	▼	42.75	-0.02(-0.05%)
20	Chevron Corporation	CVX	0.954864	▼	124.97	-0.07(-0.06%)
21	Verizon Communications Inc.	VZ	0.951243	▼	56.53	-0.06(-0.11%)
22	Home Depot Inc.	HD	0.948584	▲	213.04	0.00(0.00%)
23	Intel Corporation	INTC	0.899346	▼	50.03	-0.24(-0.48%)
24	Merck & Co. Inc.	MRK	0.855942	▲	81.87	0.48(0.59%)
25	Comcast Corporation Class A	CMCSA	0.811435	▼	44.00	-0.06(-0.14%)
26	Coca-Cola Company	KO	0.803157	▲	51.39	0.00(0.00%)
27	Boeing Company	BA	0.759836	▲	377.40	0.04(0.01%)
28	PepsiCo Inc.	PEP	0.748894	▼	130.07	-0.02(-0.02%)
29	Wells Fargo & Company	WFC	0.745134	▼	46.02	-0.01(-0.02%)
30	Citigroup Inc.	C	0.667430	▼	70.85	-0.07(-0.10%)
31	McDonald's Corporation	MCD	0.662417	▼	213.45	-0.42(-0.20%)
32	Walmart Inc.	WMT	0.645162	▼	113.79	-0.11(-0.10%)
33	Abbott Laboratories	ABT	0.622453	▼	87.38	-0.11(-0.13%)
34	Adobe Inc.	ADBE	0.608315	▼	305.45	-1.42(-0.46%)
35	Netflix Inc.	NFLX	0.571619	▼	314.08	-1.02(-0.32%)
36	Oracle Corporation	ORCL	0.567003	▼	57.50	-0.04(-0.07%)
37	PayPal Holdings Inc	PYPL	0.566229	▼	118.44	-0.19(-0.16%)
38	Philip Morris International Inc.	PM	0.548619	▼	88.30	-0.43(-0.48%)
39	Medtronic Plc	MDT	0.546233	▼	100.60	-0.20(-0.20%)
40	International Business Machines Corporation	IBM	0.532477	▲	150.05	0.37(0.25%)
41	Honeywell International Inc.	HON	0.508754	▼	172.75	-0.24(-0.14%)
42	Costco Wholesale Corporation	COST	0.500224	▼	279.99	-1.52(-0.54%)
43	Accenture Plc Class A	ACN	0.499599	▲	193.93	0.00(0.00%)
44	Union Pacific Corporation	UNP	0.495890	▲	175.30	0.00(0.00%)
45	salesforce.com inc.	CRM	0.493218	▼	156.45	-0.30(-0.19%)
46	Thermo Fisher Scientific Inc.	TMO	0.472844	▲	289.82	0.00(0.00%)
47	Broadcom Inc.	AVGO	0.461204	▼	289.95	-0.05(-0.02%)

#	Company	Symbol	Weight		Price	Change
48	Texas Instruments Incorporated	TXN	0.447244	▽	117.00	-0.26(-0.22%)
49	Starbucks Corporation	SBUX	0.445566	▽	90.19	-0.11(-0.12%)
50	Linde plc	LIN	0.444384	▲	203.38	0.00(0.00%)
51	NIKE Inc. Class B	NKE	0.441791	▽	86.49	-0.06(-0.07%)
52	Amgen Inc.	AMGN	0.440265	▽	178.18	-0.21(-0.12%)
53	United Technologies Corporation	UTX	0.428187	▽	132.23	-0.16(-0.12%)
54	NVIDIA Corporation	NVDA	0.416673	▽	167.36	-1.08(-0.64%)
55	NextEra Energy Inc.	NEE	0.408882	▲	209.73	0.00(0.00%)
56	AbbVie Inc.	ABBV	0.405642	▲	68.60	0.06(0.09%)
57	3M Company	MMM	0.401068	▲	172.61	0.00(0.00%)
58	Altria Group Inc	MO	0.380084	▽	50.40	-0.13(-0.26%)
59	Eli Lilly and Company	LLY	0.376349	▲	106.80	0.01(0.01%)
60	American Tower Corporation	AMT	0.370800	▽	205.00	-0.56(-0.27%)
61	QUALCOMM Incorporated	QCOM	0.363489	▽	74.92	-0.08(-0.11%)
62	Danaher Corporation	DHR	0.362207	▲	141.63	0.02(0.01%)
63	American Express Company	AXP	0.355029	▽	124.40	-0.42(-0.34%)
64	General Electric Company	GE	0.352716	▲	10.05	0.01(0.10%)
65	Lockheed Martin Corporation	LMT	0.352010	▽	356.93	-0.03(-0.01%)
66	Gilead Sciences Inc.	GILD	0.344448	▲	65.10	0.06(0.09%)
67	U.S. Bancorp	USB	0.332071	▽	54.97	-0.03(-0.05%)
68	Booking Holdings Inc.	BKNG	0.328260	▲	1,882.09	0.00(0.00%)
69	Lowe's Companies Inc.	LOW	0.326573	▽	102.03	-0.47(-0.46%)
70	Mondelez International Inc. Class A	MDLZ	0.320621	▲	54.89	0.00(0.00%)
71	Anthem Inc.	ANTM	0.314912	▽	300.98	-1.14(-0.38%)
72	Caterpillar Inc.	CAT	0.310424	▽	136.20	-0.03(-0.02%)
73	CME Group Inc. Class A	CME	0.296855	▲	204.85	0.00(0.00%)
74	CVS Health Corporation	CVS	0.295090	▽	55.90	-0.04(-0.07%)
75	Intuit Inc.	INTU	0.294867	▲	279.32	0.00(0.00%)
76	Automatic Data Processing Inc.	ADP	0.293557	▲	166.46	0.00(0.00%)
77	Goldman Sachs Group Inc.	GS	0.293390	▽	213.30	-0.22(-0.10%)
78	Bristol-Myers Squibb Company	BMY	0.289683	▲	43.36	0.03(0.07%)
79	Charter Communications Inc. Class A	CHTR	0.288317	▲	409.79	0.00(0.00%)
80	United Parcel Service Inc. Class B	UPS	0.288298	▽	103.00	-0.31(-0.30%)
81	Chubb Limited	CB	0.277295	▲	148.28	0.00(0.00%)
82	Becton Dickinson and Company	BDX	0.275273	▲	250.84	0.00(0.00%)
83	ConocoPhillips	COP	0.273669	▽	60.32	-0.01(-0.02%)
84	TJX Companies Inc	TJX	0.269225	▲	54.64	0.00(0.00%)
85	Cigna Corporation	CI	0.268998	▲	177.99	4.30(2.48%)
86	Duke Energy Corporation	DUK	0.262821	▲	88.60	0.15(0.17%)
87	Stryker Corporation	SYK	0.262026	▲	208.02	0.00(0.00%)
88	Celgene Corporation	CELG	0.257766	▽	90.02	-0.18(-0.20%)
89	Colgate-Palmolive Company	CL	0.254603	▲	72.70	0.00(0.00%)
90	PNC Financial Services Group Inc.	PNC	0.251930	▽	137.53	-1.30(-0.94%)
91	Dominion Energy Inc	D	0.249741	▲	76.85	0.00(0.00%)
92	Intuitive Surgical Inc.	ISRG	0.249048	▽	527.10	-1.71(-0.32%)
93	S&P Global Inc.	SPGI	0.239552	▲	241.86	1.93(0.80%)
94	Boston Scientific Corporation	BSX	0.238399	▲	42.40	0.15(0.36%)
95	Southern Company	SO	0.234877	▲	55.27	0.00(0.00%)

#	Company	Symbol	Weight	Price	Change
96	Morgan Stanley	MS	0.228372	▼ 44.23	-0.16(-0.36%)
97	BlackRock Inc.	BLK	0.227232	▲ 474.75	1.51(0.32%)
98	CSX Corporation	CSX	0.222528	▼ 70.00	-0.31(-0.44%)
99	Zoetis Inc. Class A	ZTS	0.220120	▼ 113.25	-0.84(-0.74%)
100	Northrop Grumman Corporation	NOC	0.219234	▲ 322.16	0.00(0.00%)
101	DuPont de Nemours Inc.	DD	0.215151	▼ 71.34	-0.23(-0.32%)
102	Schlumberger NV	SLB	0.214992	▼ 38.69	-0.02(-0.05%)
103	Crown Castle International Corp	CCI	0.212055	▲ 125.48	0.00(0.00%)
104	Norfolk Southern Corporation	NSC	0.209486	▼ 195.00	-0.19(-0.10%)
105	Prologis Inc.	PLD	0.209044	▲ 80.74	0.00(0.00%)
106	Marsh & McLennan Companies Inc.	MMC	0.208793	▲ 100.60	0.00(0.00%)
107	Intercontinental Exchange Inc.	ICE	0.207642	▼ 90.33	-0.44(-0.48%)
108	General Motors Company	GM	0.207464	▲ 39.50	0.02(0.05%)
109	Deere & Company	DE	0.207411	▼ 165.20	-0.41(-0.25%)
110	Ecolab Inc.	ECL	0.201592	▲ 197.28	0.00(0.00%)
111	Allergan plc	AGN	0.200755	▲ 163.16	0.00(0.00%)
112	Micron Technology Inc.	MU	0.200485	▲ 45.57	0.05(0.11%)
113	General Dynamics Corporation	GD	0.199980	▲ 183.85	0.00(0.00%)
114	Air Products and Chemicals Inc.	APD	0.199605	▲ 224.53	0.00(0.00%)
115	EOG Resources Inc.	EOG	0.199314	▼ 87.03	-0.01(-0.01%)
116	Raytheon Company	RTN	0.198295	▲ 178.57	0.00(0.00%)
117	Charles Schwab Corporation	SCHW	0.197306	▼ 42.70	-0.02(-0.05%)
118	Simon Property Group Inc.	SPG	0.196967	▲ 156.90	0.46(0.29%)
119	American International Group Inc.	AIG	0.194938	▲ 56.22	0.28(0.50%)
120	MetLife Inc.	MET	0.191383	▲ 49.72	0.00(0.00%)
121	Aon plc	AON	0.190518	▲ 194.91	0.00(0.00%)
122	Exelon Corporation	EXC	0.190345	▲ 47.75	0.18(0.38%)
123	Kimberly-Clark Corporation	KMB	0.190096	▼ 135.60	-0.14(-0.10%)
124	Progressive Corporation	PGR	0.189636	▼ 79.42	-0.56(-0.70%)
125	Waste Management Inc.	WM	0.185303	▲ 116.88	0.09(0.08%)
126	Vertex Pharmaceuticals Incorporated	VRTX	0.183398	▲ 174.13	0.00(0.00%)
127	Applied Materials Inc.	AMAT	0.182791	▼ 47.52	-0.29(-0.61%)
128	Biogen Inc.	BIIB	0.182532	▲ 231.27	0.00(0.00%)
129	Target Corporation	TGT	0.182291	▼ 87.99	-0.02(-0.02%)
130	American Electric Power Company Inc.	AEP	0.181062	▲ 90.28	0.00(0.00%)
131	Illinois Tool Works Inc.	ITW	0.181057	▲ 151.28	0.00(0.00%)
132	Illumina Inc.	ILMN	0.175539	▼ 292.61	-0.59(-0.20%)
133	Equinix Inc.	EQIX	0.173060	▲ 506.61	0.00(0.00%)
134	Analog Devices Inc.	ADI	0.172462	▲ 115.78	0.00(0.00%)
135	Phillips 66	PSX	0.172242	▲ 101.96	0.00(0.00%)
136	L3Harris Technologies Inc	LHX	0.171804	▲ 193.48	0.00(0.00%)
137	Walgreens Boots Alliance Inc	WBA	0.171284	▼ 54.39	-0.05(-0.09%)
138	Fidelity National Information Services Inc.	FIS	0.170592	▲ 129.75	0.01(0.01%)
139	Aflac Incorporated	AFL	0.168222	▼ 54.95	-0.05(-0.09%)
140	Estee Lauder Companies Inc. Class A	EL	0.167727	▲ 190.83	0.00(0.00%)
141	Capital One Financial Corporation	COF	0.167581	▼ 90.22	-0.43(-0.47%)
142	Prudential Financial Inc.	PRU	0.165587	▲ 101.02	0.00(0.00%)
143	Edwards Lifesciences Corporation	EW	0.161846	▲ 194.33	0.00(0.00%)

#	Company	Symbol	Weight	Price	Change
144	Ford Motor Company	F	0.161643	10.23	0.18(1.79%)
145	Travelers Companies Inc.	TRV	0.161391	150.23	0.00(0.00%)
146	Ross Stores Inc.	ROST	0.159423	106.61	0.00(0.00%)
147	Emerson Electric Co.	EMR	0.159199	65.29	0.00(0.00%)
148	Kinder Morgan Inc Class P	KMI	0.159044	20.50	0.00(0.00%)
149	Bank of New York Mellon Corporation	BK	0.158883	45.27	0.00(0.00%)
150	FedEx Corporation	FDX	0.158786	166.85	-0.28(-0.17%)
151	Baxter International Inc.	BAX	0.158348	83.10	0.00(0.00%)
152	Roper Technologies Inc.	ROP	0.156464	374.57	0.00(0.00%)
153	BB&T Corporation	BBT	0.156002	50.65	0.00(0.00%)
154	Dow Inc.	DOW	0.155438	51.19	-0.33(-0.64%)
155	Marriott International Inc. Class A	MAR	0.155346	137.73	0.00(0.00%)
156	Sempra Energy	SRE	0.154772	140.05	0.00(0.00%)
157	Humana Inc.	HUM	0.154338	281.67	0.00(0.00%)
158	Occidental Petroleum Corporation	OXY	0.152927	51.89	-0.44(-0.84%)
159	Autodesk Inc.	ADSK	0.152213	168.58	-0.73(-0.43%)
160	Cognizant Technology Solutions Corporation	CTSH	0.151808	65.11	-0.03(-0.05%)
161	Fiserv Inc.	FISV	0.151734	95.39	0.00(0.00%)
162	HCA Healthcare Inc	HCA	0.150781	139.48	0.00(0.00%)
163	Delta Air Lines Inc.	DAL	0.150073	61.08	0.17(0.28%)
164	Sherwin-Williams Company	SHW	0.149969	456.60	0.00(0.00%)
165	Marathon Petroleum Corporation	MPC	0.149050	55.07	-0.17(-0.31%)
166	Public Storage	PSA	0.148596	244.08	0.00(0.00%)
167	Dollar General Corporation	DG	0.148306	140.75	-0.53(-0.38%)
168	Anadarko Petroleum Corporation	APC	0.147987	73.38	0.00(0.00%)
169	Activision Blizzard Inc.	ATVI	0.140806	45.13	-0.01(-0.02%)
170	Valero Energy Corporation	VLO	0.140693	83.91	0.26(0.31%)
171	Yum! Brands Inc.	YUM	0.138569	112.68	0.15(0.13%)
172	Allstate Corporation	ALL	0.138212	101.41	0.00(0.00%)
173	Welltower Inc.	WELL	0.138138	83.05	0.00(0.00%)
174	Sysco Corporation	SYY	0.135967	70.86	0.00(0.00%)
175	Moody's Corporation	MCO	0.135932	200.89	0.00(0.00%)
176	Eaton Corp. Plc	ETN	0.135267	79.86	0.00(0.00%)
177	Constellation Brands Inc. Class A	STZ	0.135123	201.57	0.00(0.00%)
178	Williams Companies Inc.	WMB	0.133502	27.48	-0.09(-0.32%)
179	Johnson Controls International plc	JCI	0.131716	41.32	0.00(0.00%)
180	HP Inc.	HPQ	0.131032	21.58	0.19(0.89%)
181	eBay Inc.	EBAY	0.130992	40.03	-0.18(-0.45%)
182	Newmont Goldcorp Corporation	NEM	0.129764	39.28	-0.01(-0.03%)
183	O'Reilly Automotive Inc.	ORLY	0.128199	396.82	0.00(0.00%)
184	Xcel Energy Inc.	XEL	0.128147	60.77	0.00(0.00%)
185	General Mills Inc.	GIS	0.127187	52.77	0.00(0.00%)
186	Xilinx Inc.	XLNX	0.124427	122.40	-0.30(-0.24%)
187	Public Service Enterprise Group Inc	PEG	0.123432	60.18	0.00(0.00%)
188	Ingersoll-Rand Plc	IR	0.121482	124.70	0.00(0.00%)
189	Lam Research Corporation	LRCX	0.120916	197.50	-0.97(-0.49%)
190	TE Connectivity Ltd.	TEL	0.120196	89.63	0.92(1.04%)
191	AvalonBay Communities Inc.	AVB	0.117819	207.20	0.37(0.18%)

#	Company	Symbol	Weight	Price	Change
192	Advanced Micro Devices Inc.	AMD	0.117668	▲ 32.59	0.08(0.25%)
193	SunTrust Banks Inc.	STI	0.116552	▲ 65.39	0.00(0.00%)
194	Equity Residential	EQR	0.116301	▲ 77.15	0.00(0.00%)
195	Consolidated Edison Inc.	ED	0.116180	▲ 87.24	0.00(0.00%)
196	Amphenol Corporation Class A	APH	0.115844	▲ 96.64	0.00(0.00%)
197	AutoZone Inc.	AZO	0.114774	▲ 1,172.50	0.25(0.02%)
198	Hilton Worldwide Holdings Inc	HLT	0.114604	▲ 94.53	0.00(0.00%)
199	ONEOK Inc.	OKE	0.113890	▼ 68.51	-0.02(-0.03%)
200	Motorola Solutions Inc.	MSI	0.113639	▲ 168.91	0.00(0.00%)
201	V.F. Corporation	VFC	0.113250	▲ 87.49	0.15(0.17%)
202	PPG Industries Inc.	PPG	0.112022	▲ 117.51	0.00(0.00%)
203	WEC Energy Group Inc	WEC	0.110833	▲ 86.31	0.00(0.00%)
204	Alexion Pharmaceuticals Inc.	ALXN	0.110189	▲ 120.80	0.00(0.00%)
205	Twitter Inc.	TWTR	0.109752	▼ 36.68	-0.09(-0.24%)
206	Paychex Inc.	PAYX	0.109561	▼ 84.01	-0.55(-0.65%)
207	Electronic Arts Inc.	EA	0.107678	▼ 87.40	-0.10(-0.11%)
208	Discover Financial Services	DFS	0.107154	▲ 81.74	0.00(0.00%)
209	McKesson Corporation	MCK	0.107123	▲ 138.90	0.00(0.00%)
210	SBA Communications Corp. Class A	SBAC	0.105177	▲ 228.40	0.00(0.00%)
211	T. Rowe Price Group	TROW	0.105135	▲ 108.47	0.00(0.00%)
212	Global Payments Inc.	GPN	0.105005	▲ 164.73	0.00(0.00%)
213	Dollar Tree Inc.	DLTR	0.104837	▼ 107.77	-0.43(-0.40%)
214	Corning Inc	GLW	0.104347	▲ 33.39	0.28(0.85%)
215	LyondellBasell Industries NV	LYB	0.104321	▲ 85.92	0.00(0.00%)
216	Southwest Airlines Co.	LUV	0.104278	▲ 52.05	0.03(0.06%)
217	Ventas Inc.	VTR	0.102336	▲ 66.92	0.00(0.00%)
218	Monster Beverage Corporation	MNST	0.102188	▲ 63.26	0.00(0.00%)
219	Willis Towers Watson Public Limited Company	WLTW	0.102093	▲ 195.88	0.00(0.00%)
220	Zimmer Biomet Holdings Inc.	ZBH	0.101484	▲ 123.45	0.00(0.00%)
221	FleetCor Technologies Inc.	FLT	0.101336	▲ 288.83	0.00(0.00%)
222	Eversource Energy	ES	0.101218	▲ 76.77	0.00(0.00%)
223	IQVIA Holdings Inc	IQV	0.100237	▲ 155.85	0.00(0.00%)
224	Digital Realty Trust Inc.	DLR	0.100005	▼ 117.72	-0.01(-0.01%)
225	Verisk Analytics Inc	VRSK	0.099688	▲ 151.43	0.00(0.00%)
226	IDEXX Laboratories Inc.	IDXX	0.099286	▲ 286.50	1.81(0.64%)
227	T-Mobile US Inc.	TMUS	0.098033	▼ 77.10	-0.33(-0.43%)
228	Cummins Inc.	CMI	0.097196	▲ 172.80	0.00(0.00%)
229	Ball Corporation	BLL	0.096754	▲ 70.70	0.00(0.00%)
230	Cerner Corporation	CERN	0.096310	▲ 72.83	0.00(0.00%)
231	Tyson Foods Inc. Class A	TSN	0.095957	▲ 80.81	0.01(0.01%)
232	DTE Energy Company	DTE	0.095735	▲ 128.79	0.00(0.00%)
233	PACCAR Inc	PCAR	0.095611	▲ 69.33	0.00(0.00%)
234	IHS Markit Ltd.	INFO	0.095283	▲ 65.05	0.00(0.00%)
235	Regeneron Pharmaceuticals Inc.	REGN	0.095022	▲ 298.11	0.00(0.00%)
236	TransDigm Group Incorporated	TDG	0.095006	▲ 483.59	0.00(0.00%)
237	Fortive Corp.	FTV	0.093780	▲ 78.51	0.00(0.00%)
238	Edison International	EIX	0.092245	▲ 70.17	0.00(0.00%)
239	Synchrony Financial	SYF	0.092014	▲ 35.05	0.00(0.00%)

#	Company	Symbol	Weight	Price	Change
240	VeriSign Inc.	VRSN	0.091278	214.21	0.00(0.00%)
241	Pioneer Natural Resources Company	PXD	0.091248	138.00	-0.07(-0.05%)
242	M&T Bank Corporation	MTB	0.090134	162.87	0.00(0.00%)
243	Archer-Daniels-Midland Company	ADM	0.090088	40.25	0.00(0.00%)
244	Total System Services Inc.	TSS	0.089292	133.00	0.45(0.34%)
245	Agilent Technologies Inc.	A	0.089089	68.69	-0.01(-0.01%)
246	PPL Corporation	PPL	0.089081	30.30	0.13(0.43%)
247	FirstEnergy Corp.	FE	0.088735	43.49	0.00(0.00%)
248	Realty Income Corporation	O	0.088727	68.74	0.00(0.00%)
249	Cintas Corporation	CTAS	0.088636	257.85	0.00(0.00%)
250	KLA Corporation	KLAC	0.088086	131.95	-0.01(-0.01%)
251	Microchip Technology Incorporated	MCHP	0.088078	92.31	0.00(0.00%)
252	Centene Corporation	CNC	0.087881	52.09	-0.57(-1.08%)
253	Parker-Hannifin Corporation	PH	0.086628	169.61	0.00(0.00%)
254	Stanley Black & Decker Inc.	SWK	0.086544	143.55	0.00(0.00%)
255	United Airlines Holdings Inc.	UAL	0.086216	93.50	-0.33(-0.35%)
256	State Street Corporation	STT	0.085340	60.00	-0.08(-0.13%)
257	American Water Works Company Inc.	AWK	0.084872	114.98	0.00(0.00%)
258	Cadence Design Systems Inc.	CDNS	0.084429	73.00	0.08(0.11%)
259	Hartford Financial Services Group Inc.	HIG	0.083276	57.11	0.00(0.00%)
260	Clorox Company	CLX	0.083135	161.86	0.00(0.00%)
261	MSCI Inc. Class A	MSCI	0.082900	240.98	0.00(0.00%)
262	Mettler-Toledo International Inc.	MTD	0.082491	813.85	0.00(0.00%)
263	Aptiv PLC	APTV	0.082451	81.68	1.59(1.99%)
264	Ulta Beauty Inc	ULTA	0.082163	357.99	0.99(0.28%)
265	Align Technology Inc.	ALGN	0.081966	279.95	-1.26(-0.45%)
266	Hershey Company	HSY	0.081563	145.18	0.00(0.00%)
267	Synopsys Inc.	SNPS	0.081444	134.99	0.00(0.00%)
268	Fifth Third Bancorp	FITB	0.081299	27.94	0.00(0.00%)
269	Ameriprise Financial Inc.	AMP	0.081278	149.50	0.84(0.57%)
270	Entergy Corporation	ETR	0.080992	105.60	0.00(0.00%)
271	AMETEK Inc.	AME	0.080955	88.71	0.00(0.00%)
272	Boston Properties Inc.	BXP	0.080596	128.07	0.00(0.00%)
273	Northern Trust Corporation	NTRS	0.080558	92.86	0.00(0.00%)
274	Corteva Inc	CTVA	0.080105	27.99	0.60(2.19%)
275	Essex Property Trust Inc.	ESS	0.079714	298.76	3.86(1.31%)
276	Concho Resources Inc.	CXO	0.079400	101.62	0.00(0.00%)
277	Hewlett Packard Enterprise Co.	HPE	0.079400	14.84	0.00(0.00%)
278	McCormick & Company Incorporated	MKC	0.078556	158.75	0.00(0.00%)
279	Kraft Heinz Company	KHC	0.077338	31.60	0.06(0.19%)
280	Royal Caribbean Cruises Ltd.	RCL	0.076247	110.15	0.00(0.00%)
281	Republic Services Inc.	RSG	0.075908	87.11	0.00(0.00%)
282	Rockwell Automation Inc.	ROK	0.075723	159.95	0.00(0.00%)
283	Ameren Corporation	AEE	0.075514	76.78	0.80(1.05%)
284	Halliburton Company	HAL	0.075484	21.68	-0.07(-0.32%)
285	Church & Dwight Co. Inc.	CHD	0.075385	75.52	0.00(0.00%)
286	Weyerhaeuser Company	WY	0.074783	25.10	0.01(0.02%)
287	Chipotle Mexican Grill Inc.	CMG	0.074412	746.43	-0.09(-0.01%)

#	Company	Symbol	Weight	Price	Change
288	Amcor PLC	AMCR	0.073607	11.27	0.00(0.00%)
289	Carnival Corporation	CCL	0.072694	45.09	0.00(0.00%)
290	CBS Corporation Class B	CBS	0.072630	50.70	0.00(0.00%)
291	Vulcan Materials Company	VMC	0.072440	136.01	0.00(0.00%)
292	Omnicom Group Inc	OMC	0.072065	79.76	0.00(0.00%)
293	ResMed Inc.	RMD	0.071509	123.46	0.00(0.00%)
294	Laboratory Corporation of America Holdings	LH	0.070407	173.24	0.00(0.00%)
295	Kroger Co.	KR	0.070247	21.62	-0.07(-0.32%)
296	ANSYS Inc.	ANSS	0.070014	208.10	0.00(0.00%)
297	KeyCorp	KEY	0.069838	17.58	0.13(0.74%)
298	Fastenal Company	FAST	0.069455	30.01	-0.36(-1.19%)
299	Maxim Integrated Products Inc.	MXIM	0.069263	62.08	0.00(0.00%)
300	Best Buy Co. Inc.	BBY	0.068817	74.71	0.00(0.00%)
301	International Paper Company	IP	0.068642	43.24	0.00(0.00%)
302	Nucor Corporation	NUE	0.068424	57.60	0.89(1.57%)
303	Arthur J. Gallagher & Co.	AJG	0.067788	91.81	0.00(0.00%)
304	CMS Energy Corporation	CMS	0.067453	58.26	0.00(0.00%)
305	Equifax Inc.	EFX	0.067315	137.38	0.08(0.06%)
306	Keysight Technologies Inc	KEYS	0.065719	87.40	-0.06(-0.07%)
307	Cincinnati Financial Corporation	CINF	0.065537	106.45	-0.29(-0.27%)
308	Cooper Companies Inc.	COO	0.065500	331.52	0.03(0.01%)
309	CBRE Group Inc. Class A	CBRE	0.065296	52.11	0.00(0.00%)
310	Citizens Financial Group Inc.	CFG	0.065194	36.80	-0.03(-0.08%)
311	Alexandria Real Estate Equities Inc.	ARE	0.064904	142.20	0.62(0.44%)
312	Diamondback Energy Inc.	FANG	0.064117	104.61	0.00(0.00%)
313	Expedia Group Inc.	EXPE	0.064074	136.68	1.58(1.17%)
314	First Republic Bank	FRC	0.063985	98.00	0.96(0.99%)
315	Freeport-McMoRan Inc.	FCX	0.063965	11.50	0.01(0.09%)
316	Teleflex Incorporated	TFX	0.063206	335.05	0.00(0.00%)
317	Principal Financial Group Inc.	PFG	0.062564	59.97	0.60(1.01%)
318	Copart Inc.	CPRT	0.062182	77.51	0.00(0.00%)
319	Broadridge Financial Solutions Inc.	BR	0.062153	133.12	0.00(0.00%)
320	HCP Inc.	HCP	0.061953	31.74	0.00(0.00%)
321	Waters Corporation	WAT	0.061369	213.72	0.00(0.00%)
322	D.R. Horton Inc.	DHI	0.061130	45.00	0.00(0.00%)
323	Hess Corporation	HES	0.060954	60.65	0.04(0.07%)
324	Western Digital Corporation	WDC	0.060855	52.46	0.00(0.00%)
325	Darden Restaurants Inc.	DRI	0.060846	124.41	0.00(0.00%)
326	Regions Financial Corporation	RF	0.060787	15.13	0.00(0.00%)
327	DXC Technology Co.	DXC	0.060756	55.63	-0.30(-0.54%)
328	Evergy Inc.	EVRG	0.060363	60.79	0.00(0.00%)
329	Gartner Inc.	IT	0.060248	165.79	0.00(0.00%)
330	Loews Corporation	L	0.059782	53.84	0.00(0.00%)
331	CenterPoint Energy Inc.	CNP	0.058639	28.64	0.00(0.00%)
332	Symantec Corporation	SYMC	0.058324	22.26	-0.01(-0.04%)
333	WellCare Health Plans Inc.	WCG	0.058324	284.01	-2.86(-1.00%)
334	MGM Resorts International	MGM	0.058230	28.79	0.20(0.70%)
335	Huntington Bancshares Incorporated	HBAN	0.058146	13.89	0.01(0.07%)

#	Company	Symbol	Weight	Price	Change
336	NetApp Inc.	NTAP	0.058099	59.42	0.00(0.00%)
337	CarMax Inc.	KMX	0.057888	84.80	-0.04(-0.05%)
338	Xylem Inc.	XYL	0.057874	81.67	0.80(0.99%)
339	Incyte Corporation	INCY	0.057795	80.54	0.00(0.00%)
340	Arista Networks Inc.	ANET	0.057634	282.50	-0.24(-0.08%)
341	Skyworks Solutions Inc.	SWKS	0.057523	80.51	-0.81(-1.00%)
342	International Flavors & Fragrances Inc.	IFF	0.057291	142.43	0.00(0.00%)
343	Genuine Parts Company	GPC	0.057073	95.10	-0.08(-0.08%)
344	Kellogg Company	K	0.057028	56.58	0.00(0.00%)
345	Dover Corporation	DOV	0.056789	98.12	0.00(0.00%)
346	Extra Space Storage Inc.	EXR	0.056641	108.69	0.00(0.00%)
347	MarketAxess Holdings Inc.	MKTX	0.056517	367.03	0.00(0.00%)
348	Conagra Brands Inc.	CAG	0.056172	28.59	-0.31(-1.07%)
349	Martin Marietta Materials Inc.	MLM	0.055664	224.32	0.00(0.00%)
350	Mid-America Apartment Communities Inc.	MAA	0.055387	119.43	0.38(0.32%)
351	AmerisourceBergen Corporation	ABC	0.054871	85.52	0.00(0.00%)
352	Celanese Corporation	CE	0.054646	107.06	0.00(0.00%)
353	American Airlines Group Inc.	AAL	0.054585	33.10	0.02(0.06%)
354	Akamai Technologies Inc.	AKAM	0.054139	83.45	0.00(0.00%)
355	Lincoln National Corporation	LNC	0.053999	65.88	0.00(0.00%)
356	Lennar Corporation Class A	LEN	0.053951	46.25	-0.02(-0.04%)
357	Quest Diagnostics Incorporated	DGX	0.053915	99.28	0.00(0.00%)
358	Tractor Supply Company	TSCO	0.053858	113.69	1.22(1.08%)
359	DENTSPLY SIRONA Inc.	XRAY	0.053612	56.67	0.00(0.00%)
360	Cardinal Health Inc.	CAH	0.053608	44.79	-0.20(-0.44%)
361	Take-Two Interactive Software Inc.	TTWO	0.052936	116.06	0.00(0.00%)
362	J.M. Smucker Company	SJM	0.052796	114.30	0.00(0.00%)
363	Host Hotels & Resorts Inc.	HST	0.052791	17.67	0.00(0.00%)
364	UDR Inc.	UDR	0.052487	45.44	0.01(0.02%)
365	Wynn Resorts Limited	WYNN	0.052312	133.84	-0.81(-0.60%)
366	Hologic Inc.	HOLX	0.052163	48.27	0.00(0.00%)
367	Fox Corporation Class A	FOXA	0.051593	36.43	0.00(0.00%)
368	Citrix Systems Inc.	CTXS	0.051522	101.21	0.00(0.00%)
369	Expeditors International of Washington Inc.	EXPD	0.050997	74.98	0.00(0.00%)
370	Atmos Energy Corporation	ATO	0.050708	107.27	0.00(0.00%)
371	Hasbro Inc.	HAS	0.050555	107.65	-0.01(-0.01%)
372	Cboe Global Markets Inc	CBOE	0.050466	114.94	0.03(0.02%)
373	Fortinet Inc.	FTNT	0.050214	87.99	0.63(0.72%)
374	Varian Medical Systems Inc.	VAR	0.049468	132.80	0.00(0.00%)
375	Seagate Technology PLC	STX	0.048884	47.30	0.00(0.00%)
376	W.W. Grainger Inc.	GWW	0.048265	267.22	0.00(0.00%)
377	Duke Realty Corporation	DRE	0.048118	32.96	0.00(0.00%)
378	Nasdaq Inc.	NDAQ	0.048110	101.50	-0.23(-0.23%)
379	Alliant Energy Corp	LNT	0.048086	49.93	0.00(0.00%)
380	Baker Hughes a GE Company Class A	BHGE	0.047876	23.03	-0.53(-2.25%)
381	Kansas City Southern	KSU	0.047579	118.25	-5.18(-4.20%)
382	ABIOMED Inc.	ABMD	0.047449	260.00	-0.47(-0.18%)
383	AES Corporation	AES	0.046503	17.22	0.00(0.00%)

#	Company	Symbol	Weight	Price	Change
384	Masco Corporation	MAS	0.046387	▲ 38.49	0.64(1.69%)
385	Advance Auto Parts Inc.	AAP	0.046022	▲ 156.93	0.00(0.00%)
386	Textron Inc.	TXT	0.045839	▲ 49.14	0.00(0.00%)
387	E*TRADE Financial Corporation	ETFC	0.045807	▲ 47.84	0.49(1.03%)
388	Universal Health Services Inc. Class B	UHS	0.045272	▲ 132.63	0.00(0.00%)
389	C.H. Robinson Worldwide Inc.	CHRW	0.045269	▲ 83.65	0.00(0.00%)
390	Westinghouse Air Brake Technologies	WAB	0.045228	▲ 70.06	0.00(0.00%)
391	SVB Financial Group	SIVB	0.045175	▲ 222.19	2.88(1.31%)
392	Vornado Realty Trust	VNO	0.045175	▲ 63.92	0.00(0.00%)
393	FMC Corporation	FMC	0.045153	▲ 83.37	0.00(0.00%)
394	Marathon Oil Corporation	MRO	0.044953	▲ 13.66	0.00(0.00%)
395	Hormel Foods Corporation	HRL	0.044926	▼ 41.02	-0.24(-0.58%)
396	Regency Centers Corporation	REG	0.044625	▲ 65.03	0.02(0.02%)
397	Comerica Incorporated	CMA	0.044534	▲ 70.67	0.00(0.00%)
398	NiSource Inc	NI	0.044095	▲ 29.20	0.00(0.00%)
399	CenturyLink Inc.	CTL	0.043976	▼ 11.35	-0.02(-0.18%)
400	Raymond James Financial Inc.	RJF	0.043808	▲ 84.82	0.00(0.00%)
401	Jack Henry & Associates Inc.	JKHY	0.043718	▲ 141.60	0.00(0.00%)
402	Eastman Chemical Company	EMN	0.043337	▲ 78.80	0.12(0.15%)
403	CF Industries Holdings Inc.	CF	0.043115	▲ 47.16	0.00(0.00%)
404	Pinnacle West Capital Corporation	PNW	0.042942	▲ 93.59	0.00(0.00%)
405	Devon Energy Corporation	DVN	0.042899	▲ 26.34	0.00(0.00%)
406	Franklin Resources Inc.	BEN	0.042895	▲ 35.51	0.00(0.00%)
407	Norwegian Cruise Line Holdings Ltd.	NCLH	0.042798	▲ 48.81	0.21(0.43%)
408	TechnipFMC Plc	FTI	0.042607	▲ 25.11	0.00(0.00%)
409	Viacom Inc. Class B	VIAB	0.042472	▲ 30.49	0.00(0.00%)
410	PerkinElmer Inc.	PKI	0.042322	▲ 93.83	0.00(0.00%)
411	Henry Schein Inc.	HSIC	0.041569	▲ 67.50	0.00(0.00%)
412	Allegion PLC	ALLE	0.041137	▲ 107.59	0.00(0.00%)
413	Discovery Inc. Class C	DISCK	0.041022	▲ 29.00	0.00(0.00%)
414	Everest Re Group Ltd.	RE	0.040734	▲ 252.01	0.00(0.00%)
415	Arconic Inc.	ARNC	0.040359	▲ 25.18	0.00(0.00%)
416	Noble Energy Inc.	NBL	0.040348	▲ 21.19	0.00(0.00%)
417	Molson Coors Brewing Company Class B	TAP	0.040281	▼ 54.42	-0.17(-0.31%)
418	Tiffany & Co.	TIF	0.040197	▲ 92.67	0.00(0.00%)
419	Lamb Weston Holdings Inc.	LW	0.039885	▲ 68.57	0.00(0.00%)
420	United Rentals Inc.	URI	0.039595	▼ 118.88	-0.10(-0.08%)
421	Jacobs Engineering Group Inc.	JEC	0.039380	▼ 83.89	-0.02(-0.02%)
422	Huntington Ingalls Industries Inc.	HII	0.039283	▲ 230.02	0.00(0.00%)
423	Garmin Ltd.	GRMN	0.039216	▲ 81.08	0.00(0.00%)
424	Cabot Oil & Gas Corporation	COG	0.039066	▲ 22.32	0.00(0.00%)
425	Avery Dennison Corporation	AVY	0.039045	▲ 113.86	0.00(0.00%)
426	Federal Realty Investment Trust	FRT	0.038787	▲ 127.87	0.00(0.00%)
427	Mohawk Industries Inc.	MHK	0.038555	▲ 152.98	0.00(0.00%)
428	Whirlpool Corporation	WHR	0.037917	▲ 148.19	0.00(0.00%)
429	NRG Energy Inc.	NRG	0.037697	▲ 35.14	0.00(0.00%)
430	Torchmark Corporation	TMK	0.037663	▲ 91.04	0.00(0.00%)
431	Juniper Networks Inc.	JNPR	0.037298	▼ 27.00	-0.02(-0.07%)

#	Company	Symbol	Weight	Price	Change
432	Brown-Forman Corporation Class B	BF.B	0.036996	55.66	0.00(0.00%)
433	DISH Network Corporation Class A	DISH	0.036785	40.89	0.00(0.00%)
434	Packaging Corporation of America	PKG	0.036504	99.90	0.00(0.00%)
435	Mylan N.V.	MYL	0.036398	18.14	0.04(0.22%)
436	Western Union Company	WU	0.036222	20.30	-0.10(-0.49%)
437	WestRock Company	WRK	0.035575	36.23	0.00(0.00%)
438	Apache Corporation	APA	0.035420	23.95	-0.08(-0.33%)
439	Tapestry Inc.	TPR	0.035310	29.92	-0.38(-1.25%)
440	Qorvo Inc.	QRVO	0.035072	71.29	0.00(0.00%)
441	F5 Networks Inc.	FFIV	0.035010	147.97	0.00(0.00%)
442	Zions Bancorporation N.A.	ZION	0.034956	46.10	0.00(0.00%)
443	Interpublic Group of Companies Inc.	IPG	0.034621	22.80	0.00(0.00%)
444	Iron Mountain Inc.	IRM	0.034561	30.25	0.19(0.63%)
445	PulteGroup Inc.	PHM	0.034536	33.23	0.00(0.00%)
446	J.B. Hunt Transport Services Inc.	JBHT	0.033848	104.22	0.48(0.46%)
447	Snap-on Incorporated	SNA	0.033801	150.00	0.00(0.00%)
448	Mosaic Company	MOS	0.033418	24.22	0.00(0.00%)
449	Nielsen Holdings Plc	NLSN	0.033221	23.50	0.00(0.00%)
450	BorgWarner Inc.	BWA	0.032522	40.65	0.61(1.52%)
451	LKQ Corporation	LKQ	0.032312	24.94	0.00(0.00%)
452	Kohl's Corporation	KSS	0.032146	49.15	-0.18(-0.36%)
453	National Oilwell Varco Inc.	NOV	0.031862	20.99	0.00(0.00%)
454	Invesco Ltd.	IVZ	0.031778	19.77	0.00(0.00%)
455	Apartment Investment and Management	AIV	0.031560	49.70	0.08(0.16%)
456	Campbell Soup Company	CPB	0.031361	42.00	0.73(1.77%)
457	Albemarle Corporation	ALB	0.031315	74.00	-0.47(-0.63%)
458	Alaska Air Group Inc.	ALK	0.031217	63.11	-0.38(-0.60%)
459	HollyFrontier Corporation	HFC	0.030861	48.53	0.00(0.00%)
460	Fortune Brands Home & Security Inc.	FBHS	0.030681	53.65	0.00(0.00%)
461	Kimco Realty Corporation	KIM	0.030484	17.76	-0.13(-0.73%)
462	Alliance Data Systems Corporation	ADS	0.029596	151.56	0.00(0.00%)
463	FLIR Systems Inc.	FLIR	0.029012	54.05	0.00(0.00%)
464	SL Green Realty Corp.	SLG	0.028499	81.47	0.00(0.00%)
465	DaVita Inc.	DVA	0.028456	56.05	0.00(0.00%)
466	Unum Group	UNM	0.028269	32.95	0.00(0.00%)
467	Xerox Corporation	XRX	0.028106	34.35	0.06(0.17%)
468	Robert Half International Inc.	RHI	0.028102	57.64	0.00(0.00%)
469	Assurant Inc.	AIZ	0.027679	111.16	0.00(0.00%)
470	Sealed Air Corporation	SEE	0.027185	43.38	0.20(0.46%)
471	PVH Corp.	PVH	0.026646	88.25	0.00(0.00%)
472	Flowserve Corporation	FLS	0.026451	51.28	0.00(0.00%)
473	People's United Financial Inc.	PBCT	0.026116	16.40	0.07(0.43%)
474	Macy's Inc	M	0.025970	22.01	-0.09(-0.41%)
475	Perrigo Co. Plc	PRGO	0.025553	51.56	0.00(0.00%)
476	A. O. Smith Corporation	AOS	0.025061	43.58	0.00(0.00%)
477	Ralph Lauren Corporation Class A	RL	0.024330	110.27	0.00(0.00%)
478	Pentair plc	PNR	0.024069	37.38	0.00(0.00%)
479	Hanesbrands Inc.	HBI	0.023978	16.53	0.00(0.00%)

#	Company	Symbol	Weight	Price	Change
480	L Brands Inc.	LB	0.023804	▲ 25.84	0.00(0.00%)
481	Fox Corporation Class B	FOX	0.023536	▲ 36.45	0.00(0.00%)
482	Harley-Davidson Inc.	HOG	0.023496	▲ 34.85	0.00(0.00%)
483	Newell Brands Inc	NWL	0.022810	▲ 14.43	0.10(0.70%)
484	H&R Block Inc.	HRB	0.022699	▲ 28.19	0.17(0.61%)
485	Jefferies Financial Group Inc.	JEF	0.022145	▲ 20.97	0.00(0.00%)
486	Rollins Inc.	ROL	0.022137	▲ 37.82	0.00(0.00%)
487	Quanta Services Inc.	PWR	0.022052	▲ 37.84	0.00(0.00%)
488	Capri Holdings Limited	CPRI	0.021973	▲ 36.33	0.00(0.00%)
489	Nektar Therapeutics	NKTR	0.021897	▼ 31.51	-0.46(-1.44%)
490	Helmerich & Payne Inc.	HP	0.021684	▼ 51.00	-0.28(-0.55%)
491	Leggett & Platt Incorporated	LEG	0.020575	▲ 39.87	0.24(0.61%)
492	News Corporation Class A	NWSA	0.020022	▲ 13.14	0.00(0.00%)
493	Cimarex Energy Co.	XEC	0.019920	▲ 49.41	0.00(0.00%)
494	Under Armour Inc. Class A	UAA	0.019733	▼ 26.91	-0.04(-0.15%)
495	Foot Locker Inc.	FL	0.019543	▲ 42.38	0.34(0.81%)
496	Discovery Inc. Class A	DISCA	0.019231	▼ 31.41	-0.05(-0.16%)
497	IPG Photonics Corporation	IPGP	0.018596	▲ 131.60	0.00(0.00%)
498	Affiliated Managers Group Inc.	AMG	0.018568	▲ 88.37	0.00(0.00%)
499	TripAdvisor Inc.	TRIP	0.018556	▲ 44.87	0.00(0.00%)
500	Under Armour Inc. Class C	UA	0.017719	▲ 23.95	0.00(0.00%)
501	Gap Inc.	GPS	0.016046	▲ 18.78	0.00(0.00%)
502	Macerich Company	MAC	0.013957	▲ 32.26	0.00(0.00%)
503	Coty Inc. Class A	COTY	0.013352	▲ 11.07	0.00(0.00%)
504	Nordstrom Inc.	JWN	0.013287	▼ 29.58	-0.14(-0.47%)
505	News Corporation Class B	NWS	0.006165	▲ 13.51	0.00(0.00%)

Source: SlickChart.com

Appendix 23 List of FTSE100 companies (07/19/2019)

Symbol	Name	Last Price	Volume	Change	% Change	Market Cap
RDSA.L	ROYAL DUTCH SHELL PLC A	2,539.00	5,579,640	18.00	0.71%	205,086,195,712
RDSB.L	ROYAL DUTCH SHELL PLC B	2,542.50	2,923,556	11.50	0.45%	204,557,615,104
HSBA.L	HSBC HOLDINGS PLC	662.70	15,210,998	1.30	0.20%	134,410,805,248
ULVR.L	UNILEVER PLC	5,011.00	1,945,150	-54.00	-1.07%	131,701,620,736
BP.L	BP PLC	517.70	22,698,580	2.00	0.39%	105,570,418,688
BHP.L	BHP GROUP PLC ORD $0.50	2,028.50	2,307,631	31.30	1.57%	102,581,248,000
AZN.L	ASTRAZENECA PLC ORD	6,390.00	1,610,130	-12.00	-0.19%	83,822,739,456
GSK.L	GLAXOSMITHKLINE PLC	1,646.40	4,198,372	-3.40	-0.21%	82,124,898,304
RIO.L	RIO TINTO PLC	4,851.00	2,304,757	71.00	1.49%	82,116,272,128
DGE.L	DIAGEO PLC	3,387.00	2,942,895	-12.50	-0.37%	80,337,272,832
BATS.L	BRITISH AMERICAN TOBACCO PLC	3,093.00	2,997,901	-11.50	-0.37%	70,947,233,792
RB.L	RECKITT BENCKISER GROUP PLC	6,583.00	850,422	-60.00	-0.90%	46,675,378,176
PRU.L	PRUDENTIAL PLC	1,715.50	2,726,018	-4.00	-0.23%	44,599,570,432
LLOY.L	LLOYDS BANKING GROUP PLC	56.79	117,422,670	-0.60	-1.05%	40,080,621,568
REL.L	RELX PLC	1,940.00	2,251,601	5.00	0.26%	37,747,744,768
GLEN.L	GLENCORE PLC	272.25	28,112,046	2.60	0.96%	37,140,889,600
VOD.L	VODAFONE GROUP PLC	129.34	71,517,356	2.44	1.92%	34,568,830,976
AAL.L	ANGLO AMERICAN PLC	2,234.00	2,986,650	49.50	2.27%	31,389,489,152
CPG.L	COMPASS GROUP PLC	1,961.50	1,541,918	9.50	0.49%	31,116,058,624
NG.L	NATIONAL GRID PLC	834.80	5,511,623	2.80	0.34%	28,484,542,464
RBS.L	ROYAL BANK OF SCOTLAND GROUP	228.10	11,525,101	-2.60	-1.13%	27,580,026,880
BARC.L	BARCLAYS PLC	155.62	21,334,908	-0.70	-0.45%	26,836,979,712
CCL.L	CARNIVAL PLC	3,512.00	515,713	6.00	0.17%	25,123,971,072
TSCO.L	TESCO PLC	238.30	11,622,361	1.60	0.68%	23,337,912,320
STAN.L	STANDARD CHARTERED PLC	713.20	4,926,999	-1.00	-0.14%	23,086,997,504
EXPN.L	EXPERIAN PLC	2,408.00	1,225,809	28.00	1.18%	21,938,374,656
CRH.L	CRH PLC	2,651.00	1,662,952	4.00	0.15%	21,203,918,848
IMB.L	IMPERIAL BRANDS PLC	2,145.00	1,833,330	2.50	0.12%	20,512,313,344
LSE.L	LONDON STOCK EXCHANGE GROUP	5,752.00	400,970	-18.00	-0.31%	20,114,860,032
BT-A.L	BT GROUP PLC	188.98	17,937,618	-0.60	-0.32%	18,752,258,048
ABF.L	ASSOCIATED BRITISH FOODS PLC	2,343.00	604,885	-2.00	-0.09%	18,548,922,368
BA.L	BAE SYSTEMS PLC	523.20	5,867,821	6.00	1.16%	16,758,253,568
RR.L	ROLLS-ROYCE HOLDINGS PLC	863.20	2,032,696	7.20	0.84%	16,520,525,824
AV.L	AVIVA PLC	419.80	4,729,564	-1.20	-0.29%	16,442,893,312
LGEN.L	LEGAL & GENERAL GROUP PLC	269.10	7,175,019	-2.30	-0.85%	16,049,851,392
SN.L	SMITH & NEPHEW PLC	1,733.00	1,132,316	-4.00	-0.23%	15,159,572,480
FERG.L	FERGUSON PLC	5,888.00	304,725	84.00	1.45%	13,573,017,600
SSE.L	SSE PLC	1,159.00	3,209,837	-5.00	-0.43%	11,924,602,880
WPP.L	WPP PLC	916.80	5,163,501	-21.00	-2.24%	11,499,330,560
III.L	3I GROUP PLC	1,116.50	1,426,805	3.00	0.27%	10,863,678,464
INF.L	INFORMA PLC	836.20	1,795,003	7.00	0.84%	10,467,552,256
AHT.L	ASHTEAD GROUP PLC	2,211.00	1,157,933	22.00	1.01%	10,262,555,648
IHG.L	INTERCONTINENTAL HOTELS GROUP	5,514.00	185,954	-5.00	-0.09%	10,037,299,200

CCH.L	COCA-COLA HBC AG	2,735.00	570,133	-9.00	-0.33%	9,929,773,056
HL.L	HARGREAVES LANSDOWN PLC	2,070.00	416,820	20.00	0.98%	9,818,403,840
BRBY.L	BURBERRY GROUP PLC	2,328.00	1,339,592	-4.00	-0.17%	9,578,788,864
EVR.L	EVRAZ PLC	645.00	1,814,779	6.40	1.00%	9,309,607,936
ANTO.L	ANTOFAGASTA PLC	934.00	2,214,398	35.40	3.94%	9,207,988,224
IAG.L	INTERNATIONAL CONSOLIDATED	450.10	5,673,585	-5.90	-1.29%	8,931,380,224
ITRK.L	INTERTEK GROUP PLC	5,524.00	255,973	26.00	0.47%	8,915,349,504
MRO.L	MELROSE INDUSTRIES PLC	183.05	8,645,684	-0.45	-0.25%	8,893,027,328
SGE.L	SAGE GROUP PLC	803.40	2,036,005	4.40	0.55%	8,729,825,280
WTB.L	WHITBREAD PLC	4,902.00	1,130,674	17.00	0.35%	8,523,646,464
OCDO.L	OCADO GROUP PLC	1,194.50	1,840,162	54.00	4.73%	8,444,398,592
SGRO.L	SEGRO PLC	751.60	1,674,210	-3.80	-0.50%	8,217,317,376
SMT.L	SCOTTISH MORTGAGE INVESTMENT	548.50	1,879,573	1.00	0.18%	8,144,018,432
SDR.L	SCHRODERS PLC	2,947.00	424,281	-21.00	-0.71%	7,986,988,544
RTO.L	RENTOKIL INITIAL PLC	419.80	2,457,794	0.80	0.19%	7,763,487,744
HLMA.L	HALMA PLC	1,993.00	1,415,036	7.00	0.35%	7,566,324,736
BNZL.L	BUNZL PLCL	2,175.00	566,027	30.00	1.40%	7,323,985,920
NXT.L	NEXT PLC	5,460.00	210,437	20.00	0.37%	7,292,648,960
SLA.L	STANDARD LIFE ABERDEEN PLC	301.90	3,408,277	1.40	0.47%	7,277,842,944
PSON.L	PEARSON PLC	882.20	2,185,736	4.00	0.46%	6,893,855,232
DCC.L	DCC PLC	6,884.00	85,914	4.00	0.06%	6,766,635,008
ADM.L	ADMIRAL GROUP PLC	2,281.00	468,678	6.00	0.26%	6,636,570,112
MNDI.L	MONDI PLC	1,762.50	1,846,825	-16.50	-0.93%	6,472,622,592
BDEV.L	BARRATT DEVELOPMENTS PLC	634.00	2,553,911	2.60	0.41%	6,447,716,864
PSN.L	PERSIMMON PLC	1,974.00	1,450,766	-4.00	-0.20%	6,287,781,888
SMIN.L	SMITHS GROUP PLC	1,586.00	515,807	6.00	0.38%	6,279,830,016
LAND.L	LAND SECURITIES GROUP PLC	845.40	1,528,130	2.80	0.33%	6,268,319,744
CRDA.L	CRODA INTERNATIONAL PLC	4,836.00	290,968	16.00	0.33%	6,221,852,672
SKG.L	SMURFIT KAPPA GROUP PLC	2,542.00	443,101	-18.00	-0.70%	6,085,928,960
JMAT.L	JOHNSON MATTHEY PLC	3,131.00	894,489	85.00	2.79%	6,059,517,952
RSA.L	RSA INSURANCE GROUP PLC	577.20	1,645,829	1.60	0.28%	5,953,472,000
FRES.L	FRESNILLO PLC	794.80	2,939,848	-18.60	-2.29%	5,856,833,536
STJ.L	ST. JAMESS PLACE PLC	1,098.00	1,317,653	-13.50	-1.21%	5,830,061,568
MCRO.L	MICRO FOCUS INTERNATIONAL PLC	1,657.20	897,322	-15.00	-0.90%	5,689,763,840
FLTR.L	FLUTTER ENTERTAINMENT PLC ORD E	6,970.00	70,846	102.00	1.49%	5,490,087,936
TW.L	TAYLOR WIMPEY PLC	165.00	6,054,622	0.10	0.06%	5,411,637,248
UU.L	UNITED UTILITIES GROUP PLC	778.00	4,430,427	13.60	1.78%	5,305,088,512
CNA.L	CENTRICA PLC	90.26	16,231,188	0.52	0.58%	5,250,514,432
PHNX.L	PHOENIX GROUP HOLDINGS PLC ORD	716.00	801,910	2.20	0.31%	5,165,259,776
AUTO.L	AUTO TRADER GROUP PLC ORD 1P	544.60	2,740,271	-5.20	-0.95%	5,056,605,184
BLND.L	BRITISH LAND COMPANY PLC	537.80	2,115,809	0.60	0.11%	5,046,360,064
MRW.L	MORRISON (WM) SUPERMARKETS	209.40	9,099,468	1.00	0.48%	5,011,004,416
HSX.L	HISCOX LTD ORD 6.5P (DI)	1,723.00	802,873	3.00	0.17%	4,967,340,032
SMDS.L	SMITH (DS) PLC	357.20	4,029,138	-6.20	-1.71%	4,898,640,896
SVT.L	SEVERN TRENT PLC	2,041.00	998,371	4.00	0.20%	4,854,681,600
NMC.L	NMC HEALTH PLC	2,300.00	498,130	42.00	1.86%	4,801,710,080

BKG.L	BERKELEY GROUP HOLDINGS	3,756.00	418,452	-73.00	-1.91%	4,785,820,160
TUI.L	TUI AG	804.00	2,232,049	39.20	5.13%	4,726,724,096
KGF.L	KINGFISHER PLC	218.60	4,671,184	-2.70	-1.22%	4,612,744,704
DLG.L	DIRECT LINE INSURANCE GROUP	335.00	3,115,694	-1.30	-0.39%	4,606,249,984
RMV.L	RIGHTMOVE PLC ORD 0.1P	512.20	1,928,282	-5.00	-0.97%	4,557,386,752
SBRY.L	SAINSBURY (J) PLC	205.90	11,101,496	4.70	2.34%	4,553,519,616
ITV.L	ITV PLC	110.20	14,777,109	0.80	0.73%	4,436,001,792
HIK.L	HIKMA PHARMACEUTICALS PLC ORD S	1,809.00	366,496	8.50	0.47%	4,382,574,080
EZJ.L	EASYJET PLC	1,100.00	2,536,640	24.00	2.23%	4,369,288,192
JE.L	JUST EAT PLC	626.20	1,020,951	10.00	1.62%	4,269,989,120
MKS.L	MARKS AND SPENCER GROUP PLC	206.10	5,666,474	0.90	0.44%	4,019,073,792

Source: LSE Market Capitalization

Appendix 24 Sector and Industry Analysis of the United States

Sectors	Market Cap	Enterpr. Value	Earning. Yield (TTM)	Net Income (TTM)	Gross Profit Margin (Quart.)	EV to EBIT (TTM)	Total Assets (Quart.)	PE Ratio (TTM)
Basic Materials	3.281T	4.126T	7.11%	118.29B	22.74%	10.06	3.317T	14.06
Communication Services	2.712T	3.983T	6.17%	95.12B	55.43%	14.29	3.831T	16.22
Consumer Cyclical	8.004T	10.20T	4.93%	285.63B	26.94%	18.70	7.167T	20.29
Consumer Defensive	5.615T	6.408T	4.28%	145.47B	27.67%	19.85	2.815T	23.37
Energy	3.855T	5.484T	8.65%	259.34B	23.22%	9.976	6.511T	11.57
Financial Services	12.03T	24.51T	9.47%	927.94B	47.15%	9.328	110.95T	10.56
Healthcare	6.497T	7.557T	4.86%	178.24B	37.83%	19.47	3.869T	20.59
Industrials	6.797T	8.888T	5.58%	261.04B	24.46%	15.78	7.263T	17.92
Real Estate	2.334T	3.492T	4.76%	69.55B	40.54%	20.14	3.010T	21.01
Technology	11.05T	12.05T	4.46%	374.14B	39.63%	20.49	4.888T	22.40
Utilities	2.079T	3.542T	6.06%	88.00B	28.34%	16.17	3.947T	16.50

Appendix 25 Stock Portfolio

SYMBOL	DESCRIPTION	QTY	PURCHASE PRICE	CURRENT PRICE	TOTAL VALUE	TODAY'S CHANGE	TOTAL GAIN/LOSS
EBIX	EBIX, INC.	1500	$16.25	$43.66	$65,490.00	- $180.00(-0.27 %)	
BSX	BOSTON SCIENTIFIC CORPORATION	1000	$21.82	$42.70	$42,700.00		
ANET	ARISTA NETWORKS, INC.	500	$66.12	$287.72	$143,860.00		
TE		1000	$27.76	$27.76	$27,755.00	$0.00(0.00 %)	- $5.00(-0.02 %)
CCEP		500	$53.91	$56.91	$28,455.00		
AAPL	APPLE INC.	1000	$194.85	$206.16	$206,160.00		
NVDA	NVIDIA CORPORATION	1000	$201.01	$171.35	$171,350.00		- $29,660.00(-14.76 %)
AMZN	AMAZON.COM, INC.	200	$1,644.13	$1,962.97	$392,594.00	- $310.00(-0.08 %)	
AOS	A. O. SMITH CORPORATION	1000	$46.05	$43.82	$43,820.00		- $2,230.00(-4.84 %)
AWK	AMERICAN WATER WORKS COMPANY, INC.	500	$91.01	$115.45	$57,725.00		
DE	DEERE & COMPANY	1000	$148.39	$165.50	$165,500.00	- $110.00(-0.07 %)	
FMC	FMC CORPORATION	1000	$81.94	$84.07	$84,070.00		
COG	CABOT OIL & GAS CORPORATION	1000	$27.33	$22.35	$22,350.00		- $4,980.00(-18.22 %)
VRTX	VERTEX PHARMACEUTICALS INCORPORATED	1000	$171.98	$173.74	$173,735.00	- $395.00(-0.23 %)	
				Total	$1,625,564.00		

Notes and Memories

Where can you find interesting stories about investments, export, and trade on the internet?

Nurbek Achilov has some resources for you!

On Blogger's platform, he runs his blog about investments, export, trade, and other issues.

Blog about investment, export, and trade in English:

https://nurbekachilov.blogspot.com/

Blog about investment, export, and trade in English:

https://nurbekachil.blogspot.com/

You can also find ideas, photos, and experiences about investments, trade and investment on Nurbek Achilov's pages on Facebook, Instagram, Pinterest, Slideshare,

Academia and LinkedIn and other accounts.

orcid.org/0000-0003-1238-6556

Kazakhstan

Tips for Travelers

Nurbek Achilov

Second Edition

200 web-sites and tools for online presence

Essential Handbook for marketing and growth

Nurbek Achilov

First Edition

Event Management

Tips and strategies

Nigel Aksel

Second Edition

Global Citizen

Thinking Beyond

Nurbek Achilov

First Edition

Greenification

Develop, Educate and Promote

Nurbek Achilov

First Edition

.